Mission to the World

By the same author:

STEWARDS OF GRACE

FIVE MAKERS OF THE NEW TESTAMENT

THE MINISTRY OF THE WORD (Lutterworth Press)

CHRISTIAN PRIORITIES (Lutterworth Press)

THE PRAYERS OF THE NEW TESTAMENT

SINEWS OF FAITH

WORD AND WORLD

ON PREACHING (SPCK)

CONVICTIONS

SURE FOUNDATION

THE NAME ABOVE ALL NAMES (SPCK)

Mission to the World

THE CHAVASSE MEMORIAL LECTURES

1981

DONALD COGGAN

HODDER AND STOUGHTON
LONDON SYDNEY AUCKLAND TORONTO

ISBN 0 340 28268 1

 Printed in Great Britain for Hodder and Stoughton Limited, Mill Road, Dunton Green, Sevenoaks, Kent by Richard Clay (The Chaucer Press) Limited, Bungay, Suffolk. Photoset by Rowland Phototypesetting Limited, Bury St Edmunds, Suffolk. Hodder and Stoughton Editorial Office: 47 Bedford Square, London WC1B 3DP

CONTENTS

I wish to express my gratitude for the kindness which I received and for the welcome accorded to the Chavasse Lectures when I delivered them at Wycliffe Hall, Oxford, in February, 1981.

In particular the friendship of the Principal, the Rev. Geoffrey N. Shaw, and Mrs. Shaw, whose guest I was privileged to be, made those days in Oxford a delight.

Sissinghurst
Kent

Donald Coggan

I

The Biblical Perspective

THERE ARE TWO reasons why I feel myself privileged in being asked to give these lectures. The first is because of the title that they bear, "The Chavasse Lectures". Christopher Chavasse died on 10th March 1962. A fortnight later I preached in a packed Rochester Cathedral at his memorial service. He had long been a dear friend. This is no place to sketch his life, but perhaps I may be allowed to commend especially to those who did not know him Selwyn Gummer's book *The Chavasse Twins.*[1] Both brothers were Blues (1907), and Noel, who died in World War I at the age of thirty-three, was awarded a V.C. and bar. Their father, Francis James Chavasse, had been Bishop of Liverpool and before that Principal of this Hall. I could wish that his *Life* by J. B. Lancelot[2] was compulsory reading for all ordinands. The man who in the early days had said to a friend: "I shall never get married. There are three things against me, a stammering tongue, a humpy back, want of money", lived to be one of the great pastoral bishops of our Church and the father of these two remarkable sons. How often I have heard Christopher Chavasse say: "My old father used to say . . ." Father was a strong influence on son – as also was Christopher's wife, Itza. She had a perfect flair for picking up Christopher's bricks – and how he enjoyed dropping some of them! – and building with them a house of peace.

My second reason for having a sense of privilege in being asked to give these lectures is that they are based at Wycliffe Hall. To this Hall I owe a great debt, and specially to such men as Ralph Taylor, affectionately known as "Puffy", who was Principal when I was here; Douglas Harrison, a superb teacher who deserves a place in Anglican history if only because he was, so I believe, the author of the post-communion prayer beginning "Almighty God, we thank you for feeding us . . ."; and Joe Fison, prophet and bishop.

The Chavasse Lectures are *Lectures in World Mission.* I have borne this fact steadily in mind, as you will observe from the over-all title and from the five sub-titles. I need scarcely remind you that the words "mission to the world" are reminiscent of the great commission in the longer ending of St. Mark's Gospel[3] "Go into all the world and preach the gospel to the whole creation." *Into all the World* is the title of F. W. Dillistone's splendid biography of Max Warren,[4] one of the great missionary statesmen of this century, a book to which I shall have occasion to refer more than once in the coming lectures.

The titles of the last three of the five lectures speak for themselves. Jerusalem stands for the home base; "Latin America" still merits the title of "the neglected continent" in spite of great advance in missionary activity in recent decades; and "China" has hanging over it a huge question mark. "Watchman, what of the night?" might be the text of anyone who ventures to speak of the future of Christianity in that teeming country.

But before we look at the missionary movement in these three areas (and you will note that I regard Britain and indeed the West as missionary areas just as much as

Latin America or China), we must take some preliminary soundings. The story of the Church has been one of mixed response to the divine commission – glorious obedience leading to advance and victory over enemy forces, and dismal failure with resultant withdrawal and disillusionment. In the opening two lectures we are concerned with the base from which we work – *Δός μοι που στῶ και κινῶ τὴν γῆν*: "give me but one firm spot on which to stand, and I will move the earth"; so Archimedes is supposed to have said a couple of centuries before Christ. What is our base? Is it firm? And is our religion relevant "for all the world"? If we are uncertain about the answers to these questions, there will not be much "moving of the earth" in the coming generations. To change the metaphor, "if the trumpet give an uncertain sound, who shall prepare himself for the battle?"[5]

In his essay on Henry Venn, for thirty years secretary of the Church Missionary Society and one of the greatest missionary leaders of the nineteenth century, Michael Hennell writes that for Venn "the litmus test of revival was candidates for service overseas."[6] It would be interesting, perhaps disturbing, to apply that litmus test to our times. If we have not had revival on the scale for which we longed and prayed, we have none the less seen in our own day many signs of the activity of God the Holy Spirit within the Body of Christ. The charismatic movement has brought renewal to individuals and churches of all kinds. The birth and growth of communities of great variety have been the means of an infiltration of new life which has been widespread. The growth in the number of ordinands, the multiplication of study-groups, the flowering of religious publications in spite of rising costs – all these things and many others besides are signs of revival in our day. How stands "the litmus test" of candidates for services overseas? We are witnessing a decline in the number of those who offer. Some of our best young men and women are offering, but the number is small, and very often the offer is conditional on its being for a limited number of years. That may or may not be right. Does this indicate – I only ask the question – a lack of abandonment, of life-commitment like that which marked the offers of earlier recruits to the missionary cause? And if so, could it be that some of those who offer are uncertain of the grounds on which missionary activity is based? "Give me but one firm spot upon which to stand . . ." There are questions here which call for serious thought. It is time that we looked at the Biblical perspective to world mission.

There is, it seems to me, only one firm point on which we can take our stand when we look at the world mission of the Church. It is the character of the God in whom we believe. What has the Bible to say about this? It will repay us to answer this question with some care, to try to look up into the face of God and to discern its lineaments, before we look out into the world or go out to meet its needs.

Frank Lake, who can well be called one of the founding fathers of clinical theology in its modern form in this generation, in a letter to me last October remarked that he had just come across a chapter in George Adam Smith's *Isaiah* entitled "The Passion of God". He went on: "Why have we been so scared of Patripassianism as to have saddled ourselves with a God who is not 'afflicted in our afflictions'?" We may answer: "Why indeed?" I remarked in my reply: "Our fear of Patripassianism owes more to Greek philosophy than to Hebrew theology. If one takes the Fatherhood of God with any measure of seriousness, it is bound to lead one to sympathy towards that so-called heresy." That was a shorthand answer to a very big question. Here one may add that

J. K. Mozley's book *The Impassibility of God*,[7] though old, is still something of a classic on this subject. That book arose not only out of the author's membership of the Archbishops' Doctrinal Commission but also, and more urgently, out of the questions which the horrors of the first World War posed with such sharp and agonising urgency. If God is a God of love – "why Passchendaele, why gas warfare, why the trenches?" These questions were not new. Job and the Psalmists had wrestled with similar problems centuries earlier, and so had the authors of the apocalyptic literature. They were to be repeated, with increasing insistence, after World War II – "why Belsen, why Hiroshima, why Nagasaki?" They present themselves to any thinking person whenever he opens a newspaper, almost whenever he listens to a news broadcast, certainly when he goes to Calcutta. If by impassibility we mean God's freedom from passions which might affect the justice of his actions and his orderly conduct of the universe, well and good. But if, on the other hand, we mean by the use of the word impassibility to posit God's inability or unwillingness to enter into mankind's griefs and sorrows and to suffer with men as they endure them, then, as Vincent Tymms put it in a terrifying phrase: "the only God left to us will be the infinite iceberg of metaphysics."[8]

The Biblical writers express themselves again and again in such a way as to present us with a God who cannot be adequately described in terms of τὸ ὀν, "that which is", but must be spoken of in personal terms, "he who is and who was" and, further and more importantly, "he who is alive". I think, for example, of Revelation chapter 1 verse 8: "he who is and who was and who is to come". He comes not only at the climax of history to wind up human affairs, but he comes in loving intervention in history at its points of crisis and agony and joy. If in the Old Testament this emphasis is seen at its clearest in such a passage as that which Frank Lake quoted in his letter to me – "in all their afflictions he was afflicted"[9] – it is only one of many passages that could be quoted. One thinks, for example, of the saying: "I bore you on eagles' wings, and brought you unto myself",[10] and of Hosea's lovely representation of God as a father teaching his toddler to walk: "It was I who taught Ephraim to walk, I who had taken them in my arms; but they did not know that I harnessed them in leading strings and led them with bonds of love."[11] There is compassion, infinite compassion, here. How right Wheeler Robinson was, writing significantly enough in 1916, to entitle his book *The Cross in the Old Testament*![12] How can you speak of God in terms of fatherhood as the Old Testament does (for example in Psalm 103 verse 13) and not posit suffering in the father's heart? How can you speak in terms of Israel as Yahweh's bride without positing pain, passion, compassion when Israel goes a-whoring after the *baalim* and forsakes her first Love? This is sturdy, preparatory Old Testament stuff for the fuller teaching of the New Testament, with its story of the passion of the incarnate Son and the love of the Father in giving Him for a world's redemption. "A world", I said; not a chosen people or a godly remnant, but a sinful world. How can you read the parable of the prodigal son without taking seriously the passion of the father during the son's absence from home? It was only recently that I came across a verse from a modern hymn by Timothy Rees which runs like this:

God is love: and he enfoldeth
All the world in one embrace;
With unfailing grasp he holdeth
Every child of every race.
And when human hearts are breaking

Under sorrow's iron rod,
Then they find that self-same aching
Deep within the heart of God.[13]

I have had my attention drawn recently to the thinking of the Japanese theologian Kosuke Koyama who takes this matter very seriously. Let me quote briefly from him: "Jesus Christ is the centre of all things, but he is the centre who is always in motion towards the periphery. He was crucified outside the gate. He affirmed his centrality by giving it up. The Lord is supposed to be at the centre, but he is now confirming his lordship by being crucified. From that uttermost point of periphery he establishes his authority."

God loves. God suffers. God *cares*. So the Biblical documents insist; and precisely because he loves, suffers and cares, he *speaks*. I sometimes think that, if a man from Mars came to earth and, finding in his room a Bible, asked me what it was all about, and further, if I were allowed only four words in which to answer his question, I would reply: "The God who speaks". That is what the Bible is about. It concerns a God who, just because he is love, could not keep silent. "He spake by the prophets." The climax of his self-revelation was in One who could best be described as the Word. He it was above all others who gave us an exegesis of the Father.[14] He it was who, occupying the place of honour and shared purpose next to the Father, drew out for us the meaning of his fatherhood, of his nature, and made plain to us what is on his heart and mind and in his will for us. He, Jesus, is what God has to say to men. The glory of the Lord has been revealed in Christ, "and all mankind together shall see it, for the Lord himself *has spoken*."[15]

We must take this a stage further. The God of the Bible is the God who *reigns*. It would be a glimpse of the obvious to say that the main theme of the teaching of Jesus according to the Synoptic records is the theme of the reign of God, the kingdom. The majesty and the range of that theme has, at various times in the Church's history, been lessened and limited by the identification of the reign of God with the Church. To make such an identification is not only to be unfaithful to the evidence in the New Testament but also to limit the range of the compassionate love of God. God's love extends to the whole of his creation – "God so loved the *world* that he gave his Son."[16] It is his purpose that his reign should extend to and be acknowledged by all his creatures. "He has made known to us his hidden purpose" wrote the author of the Epistle to the Ephesians, "namely that the universe, all in heaven and on earth, might be brought into a unity in Christ".[17]

The fact that the reign of God has already been initiated, that it is here operative in the Church, must not blind us to the end-purpose of the reign of God. In the words of Bishop Lesslie Newbigin: "The Church is the sign, instrument *and foretaste* of God's kingdom." The realisation of God's sovereignty is far from complete. The battle is still being waged. We are in the interim time. Sin and death, though essentially defeated at Calvary, still exercise their awful powers.

The Christian task, therefore, must be not to "futurise" the meaning of the kingdom in such a way as to give it an almost exclusively eschatological connotation, nor to "spiritualise" it in such a way as to give it an almost entirely individualistic application, but to maintain the tension from which the New Testament writers draw the power of their teaching. That teaching is indeed eschatological. We have a hope which will only find its fulfilment when the reign of God is consummated. But it is also, and at the same time, strongly incarnational. It is *this*-worldly. The reign of God, in its Christian sense, was initiated with the coming, the teaching, the death and the resurrection of Jesus Christ. He went into battle against the powers of darkness. His followers can do no other than be similarly engaged. Just because they serve a God revealed supremely by Christ as being a God who loves, suffers, cares and declares himself (speaks) to his world, they too go to that world, themselves to love, suffer, care and speak. In doing that, they do their tiny bit as children of the kingdom, men and women in whom the powers of the reign of God are operating, men and women of the Incarnation, men and women of the Resurrection, men and women of Pentecost, men and women of the eschatological hope. Christ "is destined to reign until God has put all enemies under his feet . . . and when all things are thus subject to him, then the Son himself will also be made subordinate to God who made all things subject to him, and thus God will be all in all."[18]

Divine purpose, the purpose of the ages, and human participation thus meet in this doctrine of the reign of God, a doctrine springing from the passion of God, a doctrine which provides both purpose and hope for his followers who are prepared to share in that passion. He who is "Source, Guide and Goal of all that is"[19] has revealed himself in his Son who is the "pioneer of life", "the pioneer and perfecter of our faith". That pioneer bids us "come, follow". He bids us "go, tell".

I turn for a moment to that passage in St. John 20[20] which tells the story of our Lord's post-resurrection appearance to the disciples. It shows deep insight into the meaning of the Church's mission. It falls into three parts. *First*, the mission of the Church can only be fulfilled by peace-full men, that is to say by people who know the peace of divine forgiveness. The reason for the lack of peace which characterised the disciples as they met on that Sunday evening was indeed "fear of the Jews". But there was a deeper disturbance than that within them, a disturbance so deep that Jesus had to repeat his greeting of "Peace". That disturbance was due to the fact that those men had abandoned their Master at the moment of his greatest need. They had all forsaken him and fled. It was lack of forgiveness that caused the greatest commotion in their hearts that night. You can only go on the divine mission if you know yourself to be a forgiven man. That always comes first. The *third* part of the story concerns the command to "take Holy Spirit". "He breathed on them and said, 'Take Holy Spirit'." This was an extraordinary infusion of divine life, a re-enactment of the Old Testament creation story of the Lord God breathing into Adam's nostrils the breath of life. Only the Spirit-filled community can be the vehicle of God's forgiveness and exercise the authority to forgive and to pronounce unforgiven (verses 22–23).

Between these two parts comes the commission to the Church, couched in terms of monosyllabic simplicity and of immense profundity. "As my Father sent me, so send I you." "As . . . so" – those are the relevant words. As the total mission of Jesus – his praying, his teaching, his preaching, his healing, his dying, his rising – had reflected the character of the God who sent him and had shown men the lineaments of God's face, so the mission of the disciples was to do the same. As he had prayed, so were they to pray. As he had taught, preached and healed, so were they to do. As he had suffered, and in suffering had disclosed the passion of a loving Father, so their lot would be to suffer and to die. As he had risen, so they were to live and witness in the power of the resurrection-life. As he had been light to the world, so were they to be. As he had been the bread of life, so were they to be – and broken bread withal. And their total mission was to be motivated, as his had been, by a driving passion to fulfil the will of the Father.

"What a waste", people doubtless said, as they looked at the limp figure on the Cross. "What a waste – and he's only thirty-three! He might have done so much if he had only lived twice as long!" They had forgotten, if they had ever heard, what he had said about a grain of wheat falling into the ground and dying.[21] And they could not look forward and see, as we can look backwards and see, the pervasive power which Calvary was to be – and has been – down the ages, to see the cathartic influence of the Cross through the centuries.

"What a waste", people say today, as they watch some man or woman burying themselves (yes, that's the verb, significantly enough, which they use!), burying themselves in some remote and uncivilised part of the world. "What a waste of gifts and training," they say, "and what is there to show for it? Year after year of toil and hardship and not a convert, very few secret disciples even. What a waste!" But wait a minute. These people who toil in Islamic countries or in almost totally unresponsive areas of industrial society, they are working in the name of the God of compassion whose face was reflected in the ministry and passion of Jesus. They are people who, in their tiny way, reflect something of the patience of God, and who, by their very persistence in the healing work of the Gospel, make some little dent in the great oppressive forces of ignorance, sin and disease.

Or here is a Christian scholar seeking to understand the meaning of Judaism or of Buddhism or of Hinduism or of Islam, seeking to understand in such a fashion as to make amends, in however small a way, for the gaucheness of our past approaches and to open up avenues for fruitful dialogue. Or here are others looking towards China, seeking to appreciate the age-long civilisation of a people who make up a fifth of the population of the world, who have in former times been the recipients of missionaries from the West some of whom have ministered faithfully and died as martyrs, others of whom have imported the worst of the marks of the churches of Europe and America. Such scholars are engaged in a huge task, big with difficulty and calling for great delicacy of approach. Is this a waste of talent or of skill, even though the visible results are very few? Or is it, rather, a reflection of the patience of a God to whom a thousand years are but as a day and who works out his purposes with infinite love and understanding.

"God so loved the world . . .". God so *loves* the world. We are servants of that King whose reign, while its fulfilment tarries long, shall surely come. Of that reign the Church is not only the foretaste (as we have seen) but also the sign and the instrument.

I have recently been reading Sir Alan Cottrell's *Portrait of Nature: The World as Seen by Modern Science.*[22] The opening chapters, in which this great scientist writes of space and time and of the celestial spheres, are in a sense coldly terrifying. He teaches us to think of the birth of our universe some ten to twenty thousand million years ago; of ten thousand million stars in our Milky Way galaxy; of more than a million million galaxies in the universe. No wonder Robert Louis Stevenson, even in his day, wrote:

> The world is so big and I am so small,
> I do not like it at all, at all!

But in the latter part of his book, when Cottrell writes of living things, of the chemistry of creation, of the art of survival, of the miracles of evolution, we find ourselves in a world in some ways much less terrifying but equally full of wonder. "Of human beings alone", Cottrell writes, "there are now over three thousand five hundred million, but this number is easily surpassed by that of eel-worms in a single meadow, or of bacteria in a thimbleful of garden soil."

Our God is the God of the galaxies and the God of the bacteria. If it is not true that his purposes will ripen fast, it is certainly true that they will ripen, his kingdom will come, his reign will be consummated. It is cause for profound thankfulness that this God deigns to take us up into his purposes. It matters little whether our part in the fulfilment of his plan be lived out in the glare of publicity or in the shades of some hidden service, whether it achieve apparent success or be labelled by men a failure. All that matters is obedience to what is implied in the mighty statement of the risen Lord: "As my Father has sent me, so send I you." Such obedience will not go unrewarded by the God of the galaxies and of the bacteria, by the God of history and the Lord of the Church, by the God whose character has been disclosed to the human race in the face of Jesus Christ.

2

A Gospel For *All*?

We said yesterday that in the opening two of these lectures we were to be concerned with the base from which we work, and we noted the principle of Archimedes – "give me but one firm spot on which to stand, and I will move the earth." We found that one firm spot in the character of the God in whom we believe, the God who loves, suffers, cares and therefore speaks, the God who reigns and sends. We must take this a stage further today, before we can begin to look seriously at the world to which he sends his messengers, as we shall do in the next three lectures.

A Church with a vigorous and full-blooded sense of mission can only draw its vigour from a full-blooded doctrine of the triune God. The soil out of which this doctrine grew was the soil of the compassion of God. This divine compassion manifested itself, among other ways, in the election of Israel. This election, so often misunderstood in terms of privilege rather than of responsibility, took place not because Israel was bigger and better than her neighbours – indeed the reverse was the case. "The Lord did not set his love upon you or choose you because you were more in number than any people; for you were the fewest of all people; but because the

Lord loved you and because he would keep the oath he had sworn to your fathers hath the Lord brought you out and redeemed you."[1] It was out of sheer compassion that Yahweh chose Israel. When she was like an illegitimate and abandoned foundling, thrown out on the bare ground kicking helplessly in her own blood, he took her and tended her like an evergreen plant – the vivid and erotic imagery is that of Ezekiel.[2] Why did the Lord lavish such care on her? It was because his compassion spilled over and extended to the whole world, and because he saw Israel as destined to be "a light to lighten the Gentiles".

This doctrine comes to full flower in the Servant Songs of Isaiah. We need only quote a couple of passages. "I, the Lord, have called you with righteous purpose and taken you by the hand; I have formed you, and appointed you to be a light to *all peoples*, a beacon for the *nations*, to open eyes that are blind, to bring captives out of prison, out of the dungeons where they lie in darkness."[3] And again: "Now the Lord who formed me in the womb to be his servant, to bring Jacob back to him that Israel should be gathered to him, now the Lord calls me again: it is too slight a task for you, as my servant, to restore the tribes of Jacob, to bring back the descendants of Israel: I will make you a light to *the nations*, to be my salvation to *earth's farthest bounds*."[4] Here, very clearly delineated, is God's concern for the world. Here is God's compassion reaching out for the salvation of all mankind.

The matter has been admirably put by David Bosch: "Mission has its origin neither in the official Church nor in special groups within the Church. It has its origin in God. God is a missionary God, a God who crosses frontiers towards the world. In creation God was already the God of mission, with his Word and Spirit as 'Missionaries' (cf. Genesis 1, 2–3). God likewise sent his incarnate Word, his Son, into the world. And he sent his Spirit at Pentecost. Mission is God giving up himself, his becoming man, his laying aside of his divine prerogatives and taking our humanity, his moving into the world, in his Son and Spirit. From this it is clear that it is the Triune God who is the subject of mission." *Missio Dei* is God going into action – God in three Persons: the Father, the fountain of sending love; the Son, the Missionary and the model and foundation of our mission; the Spirit, the continuer of the mission and the one who empowers the disciples in mission. "The name for God in action towards the world is: Spirit".[5]

This divine compassion which we have seen to be the source of the divine mission must not be sentimentalised in our thinking. It is something deeper than sympathy, though it includes that (for we dared in yesterday's lecture to speak of a God who *suffers with* his creatures). It is a compassion that goes into action and is seen at its clearest in the incarnate Christ. In choosing the passage from Isaiah 61 as the lesson for the first sermon of his ministry,[6] Jesus was outlining the essential elements of his forthcoming mission. Good news for the poor, release for prisoners, sight for blind, freedom for broken victims – these were to be the marks of the ministry of God's great Missionary. But perhaps the most significant thing about his quotation of that passage in the synagogue on the sabbath morning was the words which were *omitted* from the passage in Isaiah. To the prophet, the climax of his passage was "the day of vengeance of our God". When Jesus read the lesson, there was a deafening silence at that point. His mission was one of grace, not of judgement. And, moreover, it was a mission of grace to *all* – to the Jews if they would but receive it, but also to people of other nations, just as God's "salvation", his saving health, had come to the Sidonian widow and the Syrian Naaman, and was to come to a Roman centurion and a Syro-Phoenician woman. It was more than the congregation in the synagogue could take. *They* were the chosen people. *They* were the favoured race. The universality of God's love, the silence about divine vengeance, the idea of a God who has no favourites – this was more than they could stomach. "They leapt up, threw him out of the town, and took him to the brow of the hill on which it was built, meaning to hurl him over the edge." "He came", as St. John was to write later, "to his own world and his own people would not receive him".[7] Missionaries are uncomfortable people, and the divine Missionary was the most uncomfortable of them all. The rejection at Nazareth that day was but an illustration of Israel's rejection of God's missionary purpose for her.

The ensuing months and years of the ministry of Jesus served only to corroborate the worst fears of those who listened to him in the synagogue. There in Jesus was to be seen the Prodigal Father, prodigal in his love, acting out that love in his Prodigal Son, prodigal in his self-giving even to the uttermost. He who had been born among cattle died among brigands, and everything that happened between those two events was richly illustrative of the divine compassion. I forbear to illustrate. Read the Gospels again. Every one of them tells the tale with utmost clarity.

Bishop John Taylor, in a memorable sentence, defines mission as "discerning what God is doing in the world and trying to do it with him". It is a searching definition of mission. "Discerning what God is doing in the world" – ay, there's the rub! Can we creatures of a brief day understand the plans of a God to whom a thousand years are but as one day? Can our small minds begin to fathom the purposes of a God of infinite patience? Faber rightly reminds us that:

> The love of God is broader
> Than the measures of man's mind

and warns us that:

> We make his love too narrow
> By false limits of our own.

Let me give an instance of this drawn from the area of thought with which these lectures deal, and let me illustrate from two conferences which were held as recently as last summer, the first in Melbourne, the second in Thailand. I speak as one who was not present at either conference, and therefore what I say must be taken with reserve as being the outcome of reading and conversation rather than presence.

The first conference was a World Council of Churches conference, the third meeting of the Commission for World Mission and Evangelism, following up its second meeting in Bangkok in 1973 when the theme was "Salvation Today". Melbourne's theme was "Your Kingdom Come". Some six hundred people attended, the majority of them being from Africa, Asia and Latin America, representatives of the Third World, or, as perhaps we should rather now say, the southern, poor part of our globe. Others came from lands where persecution was the lot of those who professed the faith of Christ crucified, flesh and blood reminders of the persecution which all down the centuries has been one mark of the Christian's lot. There was no escape for the delegates from confrontation with the powers of evil. Poverty, persecution, over-population, pollution, war, misuse of political power and of the forces of nature, blatant injustice and inequality, racism, oppression, rejection – all were represented there. Could the West – to use the old terminology – which had launched the atom bomb, which kept control of the vast majority of the world's wealth while millions starved, which was cultured while adult millions remained illiterate – could the West still have a word to say to such people? And if they had, could they expect a hearing? What did it mean for a comfortable European to use the phrase "God's salvation"? What was he praying for precisely when he prayed "Thy Kingdom come"?

Let me here interpolate a few sentences about a book which I have been reading recently, for the man whose biography it is was one who felt these issues very keenly and in his person and writings anticipated many of the problems which arose in so sharp a form at Melbourne. Hugh Tinker's *Life* of C. F. Andrews[8] is not a hagiography. The writer does not shrink from depicting Andrews' very obvious weaknesses. But in this carefully documented book he draws for us a picture of a man who gave himself, with an almost terrible totality of giving, to India and to her sons and daughters in that sub-continent, in Fiji, in Africa and elsewhere. Close and intimate friend of Gandhi and of Rabindranath Tagore, he looked at India with its teeming millions and apparently insoluble problems, almost with the eyes of an Indian. But he was also a Britisher, seeking to serve India towards the close of the period of British rule (he died in 1940). He was aware of the contribution which Britain had made to India, but he was also painfully aware of the injustices which obtained under British rule, injustices to which many Britishers seemed intentionally to turn a blind eye. Even the clergy seemed infected by white racism. As long ago as 1925, on a visit to South

Africa, Andrews wrote that there was "no spot on earth where the colour bar is so rampant as in South Africa, and the Christian clergy seem to have almost sold themselves to their congregations". With men like the Viceroy, Edward Wood (Lord Irwin, later Lord Halifax), he had much in common, for Halifax was a deeply religious Anglican. With Gandhi, Andrews found himself in closest understanding, and joined him again and again in protest against exploitation of the masses by the powerful. He would have been entirely at one with Gandhi when the latter outlined the seven sins thus:

Politics without principle;
Wealth without work;
Pleasure without conscience;
Knowledge without character;
Commerce without morality;
Science without humanity;
Worship without sacrifice.

And so for that matter would Amos and Isaiah and a long line of godly thinkers down the centuries.

C. F. Andrews being dead, yet speaks. The issues over which he agonised were much the same as those that faced the delegates at Melbourne. When those delegates read St. Luke's story of our Lord's sermon at Nazareth to which I have already referred, what were they to do with its reference to "the poor, the prisoners, the blind, the broken victims of oppression"? Or what were they to do for that matter with the *Magnificat* of an earlier chapter of St. Luke[9] with its references to God's putting to rout the arrogant, his bringing down the monarchs, his lifting high the humble, his satisfying the poor with good things, his sending the rich empty away – references which sound to me much more like a Communist plan of campaign or manifesto than an Anglican chant sung by the choir at Evensong in Puddlecombe-by-the-Marsh? What were they to do? They could, of course, spiritualise it all – the poor are the spiritually poor, and the blind are those with Christless eyes. Or they could postpone it all to a future world, when God would have wiped away all tears and there would be pie in the sky for all. That might do for the pietist from the luxurious West, but it would not do for the delegate brought up in a South American favella, or for the other delegate who was a friend of the recently murdered Archbishop Romero – it would not do for them any more than it did for Charlie Andrews in his day of wrestling with similar problems in India. It would not do for the delegates who had been nourished on liberation theology, who had a right to ask whether God was now at work within the historic process and, if so, *how* he was at work and *whom* he used in the carrying out of his work, his strange work.

This, of course, was not new to Melbourne. Those of us who were at the World Council of Churches meetings in New Delhi in 1961 and Uppsala in 1968 and Nairobi in 1975 (as I was myself), and those who were at Bangkok in 1973 had heard these things before. The new element at Melbourne, so a friend of mine who was present perceived, was a growing sense of frustration on the part of speakers from the Third World, "the poor", and a growing embarrassment on the part of those who came from the Western industrial countries, "the rich". The optimism which had marked Uppsala in 1968 had gone. The realities of the world as it was at the beginning of the nineteen-eighties faced Melbourne in all their dreadfulness.

The conference held in Pattaya, Thailand, in June last year was not a conference of delegates (as was the Melbourne conference). It was a Consultation on World

Evangelisation, and the members were individuals invited by the Lausanne Committee for World Evangelisation. That is to say, it was a conference of evangelicals with a large American participation, together with observers and advisers, etc. Its theme was "How shall they hear?".

A perceptive friend of mine who was present at Pattaya felt very strongly that the readiness to see the social implications of the Gospel which was so clearly accented at Lausanne in 1974 (and which had been realistically faced at the Nottingham Conference in 1977) had faded in 1980. Only at the end of the conference was there a clear expression of the social implications of the Gospel (and that concern does appear in the closing statement). But the immediacy of the concern had faded, and St. Luke 4,16 ff. was "spiritualised". Simon Barrington-Ward, in reporting on this conference – he had come on from Melbourne – wrote of "no sense of structural oppression and no Marxist resonance . . . in place of the Marxist overtones of Melbourne there was an almost capitalist ethos of consumer research and methods of promotion". (He was referring, I think, to groups whose task it was to consider how to reach Muslims, Hindus, city-dwellers, and so on.). "We seemed blandly unaware of the chains that bound us."[10]

It would be an over-simplification to say that Melbourne presented a Gospel of political liberation and social and cultural improvement, a this-worldly deliverance from evil, while Pattaya presented a Gospel of spiritual redemption which sat loose to the present ills which cry out for remedy. There were those like Emilio Castro at Melbourne who kept reminding the delegates of the need to face the implications of the Gospel in regard to repentance and the offer of forgiveness in Christ and *at the same time* to be open to the pain of the poor. And there were those like Bishop David Gitari, of Kenya, who reminded the members of the Pattaya conference that the social implications of the Gospel must be faced realistically. But if shorthand is to be used in summarising the stance of the two conferences, the contrast which I have just made would not be far from the truth. It pinpoints the danger of an either/or approach to the subject of mission, whereas the Biblical approach is the much more difficult and demanding one of both/and. Those who out of concern for their fellow-men put their heart into improving the circumstances of life and altering the structures of society will have to learn from the Scriptures that what we are offered by God is something deeper than better living: it is life eternal. And those who make their own spiritual experience the measure of discipleship will have to learn from the Scriptures that God has many ways of making people his own. The Bible is always richer than our comprehension of God and our ability to express and live our faith. It is a sad thing when a Christian thinker allows himself to be impaled on an either/or antithesis and thereby misses the magnificence of a both/and missionary philosophy and strategy.

David Bosch, writing before Melbourne and Pattaya, dealt with precisely those matters which these conferences were to highlight. He pointed out that for many evangelicals the social dimension of the Gospel, and the involvement of the Christian in world affairs, is regarded as a supplement to be added on to evangelism, whereas in fact the social dimension of the Gospel is indeed *a part of it*, and to defect from participation in that part of the Gospel is to be guilty not only of hypocrisy but of apostasy. "Ecumenical" theology, on the other hand, has often been guilty of *reducing* the Gospel, of having a one-dimensional interpretation of history, of failing to stress the reality of sin in every man and the consequent need of repentance and conversion. "Eschatology and soteriology are reduced to ethics."[11]

It is only when the distinctive emphases and insights of Melbourne and Pattaya – we are using shorthand again! – are held together in a creative tension; it is only when we refuse the luxury of either/or and come down boldly on the side of both/and; it is only when we face willingly the double stress of Scripture on the physical and the spiritual and on their oneness in the mind of God and in his passion for the world; it is only then that the glory of the Gospel is seen in its fulness and the dimensions of the missionary task can be apprehended.

I wish in the latter part of this lecture to revert to Bishop John Taylor's definition of mission as "discerning what God is doing in the world and trying to do it with him", and to relate that "discerning" particularly to the matter of the non-Christian religions of the world. Obviously it will be impossible to do more than to touch briefly on so huge a subject in so short a time – a subject which exercises the minds of missiologists, which daily confronts the missionary who does his work in a preponderantly non-Christian milieu, and which should raise questions in our minds every time we see a mosque in our own country or come in contact with a Muslim or a Hindu.

A subject such as this is often best approached through examining the life and writings of one person who gave himself to its elucidation and exposition. Let me suggest that anyone embarking on this subject might begin by reading two books. The first is Max Warren's autobiography *Crowded Canvas: Some Experiences of a Lifetime.*[12] The second is F. W. Dillistone's *Into All the World: a Biography of Max Warren.*[13] For our purpose the latter is more important than the former, fascinating and revealing as the autobiography is. Those who have read Dillistone's biographies of Charles Raven and of C. H. Dodd know how expert he is not only in chronicling the events of the life he is writing but of penetrating the thought, exposing the mind, putting his finger on the pulse of the man concerned. He has done this supremely well in the case of Max Warren. *Into all the World* is more than a biography. The sub-title might well have been *The Life and Thought of Max Warren*.

Max was trained as an historian; he got a first class in both history and theology at Cambridge and won the Lightfoot Scholarship in Ecclesiastical History. He never lost interest in history and never ceased to ponder on the ways of God with men as he discerned (or tried to discern) them in the annals of ancient, mediaeval and modern history, or in the pages of the daily newspaper or of *The Economist*. He used to say that these journals should be read, together with the Bible, as a background and a guide to one's prayers. His approach to the Bible was, as Dillistone points out, historical rather than mystical or philosophical or typological. He was at home with the prophets who, amid the clash of conflicting cultures, discerned "the guiding hand of One who was in control of history and who was working out his purpose in history". Isaiah, Jeremiah, Habakkuk – these were his hunting grounds for an approach to modern history which took as seriously the activities of a Stalin, a Mao, a Nehru, an Eisenhower, a Sheik Yamani as the Old Testament writers took seriously the activities of a Joshua, a Moses, a Cyrus, a Nebuchadnezzar. "We will be wise", said Max Warren, ". . . to take all history seriously. This, after all, is involved if we take the Incarnation of our Lord seriously . . . Isolating the Church from history is another way of being anti-Christ." So he wrote in his last substantial book *I Believe in the Great Commission.*[14] He would often recur to his belief that God was in control of history; at the same time God was altogether beyond human control. "Christians, whatever their race, are committed to the Biblical faith that God is at work in history, that all history, therefore, is sacred history, even that which seems most secular." How he spelt that out may be seen by those who care to read Part III of his *I Believe in the Great Commission,* and specially chapter 7 of that book. He would have said his Amen to Lesslie Newbigin's assertion that "the object of God's reign is human (and cosmic) history as a whole."

What are we to make, then, of the place of the great religions in the long conspectus of the history of the world? What part have they, if any, in the strategy of God for the people of his creation? We rightly reject any view of God which conceives of him as winding up the clock of the world at the beginning of time and then, as it were, standing aside and letting his world get on with it till the clock stops. "My Father has never yet ceased his work, and I am working too." So St. John represents Jesus as saying when he defended himself against the charges of the Jews because he healed on the Sabbath day.[15] Wherever there is release from the bondage of sin or of sickness or of poverty, there we may see the creative and recreative hand of God at work. May we not see this, not only in the cases of individuals redeemed, restored and forgiven, but also on the larger canvas of nations and civilisations? Was not God at work in the thinking of a Socrates or a Plato, in the beauty of words, of design, of art, of architecture which mark the civilisation of Greece? And was he not equally at work in the magisterial system of law and order which Rome gave to the world and which has been the basis of law for succeeding generations of people in many parts of the world? Truth, beauty, order, wherever they are and through whomsoever they come, must be seen as the gift of a God who is at work in every generation and who because he is a God of *compassion* (we come back to our former word) cares for the welfare of his children. Yes, and cares with infinite patience, as he wrestles with man's stupidity and sinfulness.

Let that be granted – on the wide canvas of the passing civilisations. But what are we to say about the *religions* of the world which wax and wane, and some of which are doing a great deal of waxing today – to our amazement and discomfiture? It is comparatively easy to speak of Israel and her contribution to the world, her insight into the deep things of God and, for all her desperate defaulting from the plan of God for her as a people, her preparation of the nations for the coming of Christ. We know about the godly remnant. We know about its reduction to the lonely One upon the cross. We know about its burgeoning out – the call of the twelve, the illapse of Pentecost, the sending forth of the Church, the growth of the ecumenical Church. We know about the synagogues, those first apostles to the Gentiles. We know about the Septuagint which, read in the ears of the Gentile God-fearers, opened up to them visions of the one true God which their own religions had never been able to disclose to them. There, in Israel, disobedient as she so often was to the heavenly vision and calling, we can see something of the slow outworking of the plan of God for his world.

But what of the other religions? "My Father has never ceased his work, and I am working too." May we see this in operation not only in individuals, not only in civilisations, not only in Israel, but also in some fashion in the other religions of the world, however dimly and in however distorted a form they presented themselves to the world at their beginnings, and however dimly and distortedly – sometimes more dimly and distortedly than at the beginning – they have presented themselves to their followers down the centuries, and do so today?

Let us begin with a very modern religion. I wrote this lecture a few days after the death by shooting of John Lennon. He was a god, or something very near it, to millions of young people who had no other god to worship. So when the god died – with a hundred million pounds safely stacked away – twenty thousand of them sang hymns (Lennon's music) in their cathedral (Central Park, New York) and waved banners extolling peace, and lit candles. They prayed, many of them to a god who had no face, an "unknown god", but they prayed. Their differences of age and race and religion seemed for a brief hour to be transcended. I found my mind travelling, as I read the report, to the seventeenth chapter of the Acts of the Apostles: "God created every race of men . . . They were to seek God, and, it might be, touch and find him, though indeed he is not far from each one of us . . ."[16] Who moved them? Was "My Father still at work"? – however dimly they were conscious of his presence, and even when there was no response to him or, perhaps, even any consciousness of him at all? What was going on in Central Park, New York, that day?

Please do not think that I am engaging in any kind of sentimental universalism or pleading for a kind of syncretistic pantheism! Far from it. Certainly St. Paul was doing nothing of the sort at Athens in the passage from which I have just quoted. He was very clear on his proclamation (verse 23), very clear on his doctrine of creation (verse 26) and on his eschatology and on his emphasis on the resurrection of Christ (verse 31). But, surrounded as he was by crowds of men, some seeking God seriously, others engaged in grave theological discussion, and others in mere philosophical niceties, he was seeking to face the realities of what God was about in what, after all, was still his world. The Father's compassion went out, even in Athens, to his creatures, his "offspring" as St. Paul called them, quoting from Aratus's *Phainomena*.

It would, I suppose, be possible to take a "dismissive" attitude to all non-Christian faiths, to see them as manifestations of evil, as men's unaided fumblings in the dark, or even as Satanic distortions of truth. But this totally black-and-white approach to the matter leaves unanswered a host of questions. What has God been up to down the long centuries? What is he up to today in a world the vast majority of whose people are non-Christian, and millions of whom have never heard the name of Jesus, while tens of millions of those who have heard the Name have never had an opportunity of intelligently facing his demands or receiving his grace? What are we to make of a Gandhi whose philosophy of life and peace was so largely based on the teaching of Jesus and who, had it not been for what he saw in the so-called Christian West, might well have become a committed Christian himself? Or what are we to say about Rabindranath Tagore, mystic, poet, intimate friend (like Gandhi) of C. F. Andrews? I have mentioned two names from the recent history of India, but you could add the names of many more from that and other lands through whose work and life and writings truth came through to men and peace was shed abroad. Whence came these things, if not from the God of all compassion and of truth and of peace? To be on the lookout for evidence of God's prevenient grace in peoples and religions other than our own is not, it seems to me, to do despite to the uniqueness of Christ but rather to enhance our awed appreciation of the love of God at work in his world.

Perhaps the most constructive way of approaching the great religions of the world is to see them as the reaching out of men and women to God in prayer and worship. The form of that reaching out may be primitive and, to us, even revolting at times, something little more than a flicker in comparison to the fulness of light which has been given us in the face of Jesus Christ. But a reaching out it is – to the awe-full God who is always there first. The case of Cornelius must be taken seriously. He was a Roman, a pagan if that means a non-Christian. But the writer of the Acts points out very clearly that "he was a religious man, and he and his whole family joined in the worship of God. He gave generously to help the Jewish people and was regular in his prayers to God."[17] The angel who appeared to him assured him that his "prayers and acts of charity" had gone "up to heaven to speak for him before God". He was ripe for Peter's presentation of the Gospel. Peter began by pointing out the truth that "God has no favourites but in every nation the man who is godfearing and does what is right is acceptable to him." That undoubted fact does not lessen the urgency of presenting Cornelius with the truth as it is in Jesus; but it means that Peter, in approaching Cornelius, must do so with a courtesy and even a reverence which is due to a man who has had dealings with God.

Must we not say that millions of Muslims have had dealings with God and are having such dealings today? If that is so, the mosque in our city may present us with problems, but at least we look straight at it and do not just wish it was not there. If we were not so infected with spiritual or even imperialistic *hybris*, might we not learn from them something of the transcendence of God, and from the Buddhists, in their teeming millions, something of his immanence? We believe that in Jesus we see, as nowhere else, a reconciliation of the apparent opposites of transcendence and immanence because he was both God and man. But we are very small and he is very big, and it may be that the stance of a humble learner will prove to be the most likely position from which to see truth in all its greatness.[18]

To think big and to take history seriously because it is the sphere of God's operational activity; to handle with reverence and humility the "feelings after him" of men who, while not being Christians, are, like Cornelius, godfearing; to try to understand St. Paul's vision of all things being summed up in Christ[19] and God being "all in all", "everything to everyone";[20] to ponder on God's infinite patience and on the magnificence of One apart from whom no man can see God as Father in the sense in which Christ knew him – this is the task of those who take seriously a Gospel which "through prophetic scriptures, by eternal God's command (is) made known to all nations, to bring them to faith and obedience".[21] When we attempt that task, we had better take our shoes off, for the ground on which we tread is holy.

3
"Beginning at Jerusalem"

YOU WILL RECOGNISE the phrase which is the heading of this lecture as coming from St. Luke's account of the post-resurrection appearance of Jesus and of his commissioning of his disciples as witnesses.[1] Howard Marshall, in his great commentary on St. Luke, says that the phrase "is loosely added . . . the syntax is harsh". Its awkwardness led to a variety of emendations by scribes. The words can be read, and indeed are so read in the Authorised Version, the Revised Standard Version and others, with the words that precede them: "Repentance and remission of sins should be preached in his name, beginning at Jerusalem." But, equally well, they can be taken with the words that follow: "Beginning at Jerusalem, you are witnesses of these things." The New English Bible seems to favour the latter punctuation: "Begin from Jerusalem: it is you who are the witnesses to all this." Hans Conzelmann notes that "when Luke speaks of the *archē* in Jerusalem, it has not just a historical significance, but concerns basic principles." "The 'beginning' in Galilee (St. Luke 1,2) and the 'beginning' of the Church in Jerusalem are deliberately placed parallel to each other." "It is only here that the outpouring of the Spirit can take place. Pentecost is not only the typological foreshadowing of the mission, but also the historical foundation for it. For this reason the mission spreads out from Jerusalem in concentric circles."

Conzelmann is right. Here are basic principles indeed. Jerusalem was the place of Jesus' resurrection. Jerusalem was the place of Pentecost and the illapse of the Spirit. *There can be no mission apart from these.* "If Christ be not risen, then is your preaching vain, and your faith is also vain."[2] If there be no illapse of and receptivity to the Spirit, then is your mission vain! Resurrection, Pentecost, mission – the three are inseparable. What God hath joined together, let no man put asunder. The early Church knew this, and in the power of that knowledge went forth, conquering and to conquer.

But there is even more to it than this. Jerusalem stands for your home base, the place where you are known, perhaps where you have grown up. If you cannot witness *there*, it is vain to think that a change of place will itself make you into an effective witness elsewhere. Jesus began his public ministry in his home town at Nazareth, the most difficult of all places in which to witness – and "people marvelled at the words of grace that proceeded from his mouth."[3] It is a word of warning to all would-be missionaries.

So then, whereas the first two lectures dealt with the theological base from which those work who are engaged in mission, today we use the term "base" in a more geographical sense. Broadly speaking, it is what we still call the West, that is to say, roughly Europe and North America in large part. Perhaps we should now learn to speak of it as the North, the rich nations in contrast to the poor nations of Africa, Asia, Latin America etc. – though even that demands caution (has not Nigeria found oil?).

One thing is blindingly clear, though the point is not

always taken. It is that it would be utter disaster for anyone to go to any part of the third world who had not been disinfected of any kind of western "superiority", of imperialistic pride, or of paternalistic approach.

Mary Moorman has just written the *Life* of her father, George Macaulay Trevelyan.[4] At the end of the book she records a conversation just before his death which the great historian had with a friend. The last volume of the *Cambridge Modern History* had recently appeared. Its title was *The Age of Violence*. "Yes", said George, "the last sixty years have been an age of violence. It began with the Boer War, when the Tory Imperialists still thought it possible to expand the Empire and step up British immigration into South Africa till there was an English-speaking majority. But it did not come off. The age of Imperialism was ending. Imperialism was dying, but before it died it brought on in its struggles two terrible World Wars. It has indeed been an age of violence."

A perusal of Thomas Pakenham's stout volume *The Boer War*[5] with its story of the British army sweeping the veld clean at Kitchener's command, and between twenty thousand and twenty-eight thousand Boer civilians dying of epidemics in "concentration camps", does not make very pretty reading. Nor does the dropping of atomic bombs by Western nations on Nagasaki and Hiroshima. I mention these painful episodes merely to suggest that any emissary from the West to peoples with other backgrounds would do well to be clothed with a comely humility. The days when white bishop and colonial governor could be seen as representatives of imperial power are long gone, but they have left a legacy which has not been forgotten nor soon will be. As St. Paul said in a somewhat different context, "boasting is excluded"!

Penitence is called for, while at the same time we seek to keep our sense of historical balance by recalling great contributions made under British rule, and remembering with humble thankfulness the noble army of missionary martyrs and dedicated civil servants whose bones lie in the countries to which they gave themselves, and that in days of few drugs and few creature comforts.

We from the Churches of the West go to the developing countries as servants, representatives of *the* Servant who "accepted even death – death on a cross".[6] We do not grovel, that is not the meaning of being servants. We go as servants of Christ to stand alongside other servants of Christ where the ground is level, namely at the foot of the Cross. All of us have empty hands – hands stretched out for forgiveness, hands stretched out to receive the tokens of Christ's love in the sacrament of his body and blood, hands stretched out for strength and enabling. The colour of those hands makes no difference at all. They are all empty. And if they are empty to receive his grace in the sacrament, they are also empty to receive from one another, black from white *and* white from black.

Let me take up this last point for a moment. The curate straight from college and with his theological training safely behind him goes to his parish. He has the answers to most of life's problems – did he not get a First in his theological degree? One of the first calls he has to pay is on an old lady dying of cancer. As he goes to her bedside, he prepares something to say – after all, he has to minister to her. When he gets there, he finds someone not very learned, indeed scarcely literate. But she is what the Scots call "far ben wi' God". She knows whom she has believed and is persuaded that he is able to keep her. She is not a woman of many words, but somehow (he cannot quite explain it but he knows it to be true) she ministers to him. The young man who went to give has come away immensely enriched. He has received at her hands.

This principle works in a wider field. When I first went to the diocese of Canterbury I was conscious of a certain insularity of outlook which is one of the special temptations of an insular people. (Do you recall Max Warren's remark? – "insularity is still what it always has been, a demonic curse with power to enfeeble."[7]) I was singularly fortunate in being able to import a priest from the Church of South India who had also had wide experience of work in Africa. We organised no great meetings for him – anyway that sort of thing was not particularly his métier. We just let him loose in small groups around the diocese. We sat at his feet and learned; and how we were enriched! India taught England. White skins learned from dark. Shallows learned from deeps. We were grateful receivers.

On a still wider field the principle works. M.R.I. – Mutual Responsibility and Interdependence in the Body of Christ – was the child of the Toronto Congress of 1963. It was a healthy child – I had a share in the midwifery operation! It was intended to show the interdependence of one part of our Anglican Communion on another. Much was achieved along these lines. A list of needs was drawn up and many of these needs were met. A lot of money was involved. Much sacrificial giving resulted, and that, no doubt, did the givers good and often, not always, did the receivers good. But the dangerous part of the operation lay here – that it tended to bolster the idea of the West as the givers while the developing nations were the receivers, a one-way operation of rich giving to poor. It is, of course, true that from a material point of view the West must still give to the third world; and indeed in non-material things, in expertise (theological, medical, educational), the aid of the

West is still needed and often welcomed. We must go on giving of our best in these areas of need – to export our best in man- and woman-power is still right. But as we do so, we must keep our eyes wide open to the fact that many of us in the West tend, like the members of the Church at Laodicea, to say: "How rich I am . . . I have everything I want", and do not realise that spiritually we are "poor, blind and naked".[8] We need to learn lessons of silence and meditation from India, of exuberance and joy from East Africa, of freedom from Latin America, of endurance from nations where Christians are persecuted just because they are Christians, of forgiveness from Iran. Our prayer must be for a spirit of humility, of receptivity and of openness.

This abandonment of *hybris*, this spirit of humble openness assumes the adoption by us all of a world perspective which makes very considerable demands on us. "Jerusalem" (to revert to the terminology with which we began this lecture) is comfortable. It is set on a hill. It is secure. It has around it a wall which is not easily breached. It has behind it a history venerable in its antiquity. The comfortable course would be to remain inside it, cocooned, if may be, from the tumult of the nations which roar, which rise and fall around it. Britain, our "Jerusalem", is comfortable – yes, even in a day when the unemployment figure has passed the two million mark, when violence lurks in the streets, when income tax is high. Yes, Britain is comfortable, when you compare our standard of living with that endured by tens of millions of our fellow world-citizens. We have a police force which, with very few exceptions, cannot be bribed or intimidated. We have a press which is free to express its views. We have a welfare state which cares for us from womb to tomb. And if the fact of our being a multi-racial society sometimes disturbs our ease, we can avert our eyes from the local mosque, close our nose to the scent of curry, and think of the good old days when Britain *was* Britain and ruled the waves.

Such an outlook is for the Christian totally impossible. His must be a *world perspective*, and it must be a central part of his mission to share that perspective and to spread that way of looking at the world. Readers of Dillistone's *Life* of Max Warren (to which I have already referred more than once) will recall how that omnivorous reader paid daily attention to *The Times* and weekly attention to *The Economist.* This he did, partly to add fuel to his prayers and to make his intercessions intelligent, and partly to help him in getting and keeping his world perspective right. He died too soon to read *North-South: A Programme for Survival,* more familiarly known as the Brandt Report.[9] In fact, Max died in 1977, and it was in December of that year that the Commission which produced the Report met for the first time.

Had Max survived he would, I think, have wanted it to be compulsory reading for those who are seeking to be obedient to the divine commission – or at least he would have wanted them to read and ponder on Willy Brandt's own *Introduction* to the Report. There is much in the Report which is heavy going for those of us who are strangers to the world of finance, trade and industry. But to read the twenty-two pages of the Introduction, Brandt's own work, is to find oneself in company with a mind that is grappling with world problems with realism and compassion. With many of those problems many of us have been familiar for many years – illiteracy, for example. Of this Brandt writes: "Illiteracy . . . is a tremendous waste of human potential. Literacy . . . arouses people's consciousness and helps them participate in community life. Thus it is also a prerequisite for fighting hunger and disease." Again, writing of environmental pollution and the spoliation of earth's resources, Brandt writes: "The oil stock of our planet has been built up in a long process over millions of years, and is being blown 'up the chimney' within a few generations . . . The grave consequences of increasing soil erosion and desertification should also concern all of us. Unchecked deforestation at its present rate would halve the stock of usable wood by the end of this century (and deprive more than a billion poor people of their essential fuel for cooking) . . . It is not just a risk to the environment, it is a plundering of our planet . . ." Again, he has some fearful things to say about the madness of "the mounting spiral of sophisticated and expensive weaponry" – "we may already be arming ourselves to death". And if for you, as for me, four hundred and fifty billion dollars does not convey very much – and that is, roughly, the annual military bill for armaments! – Brandt kindly breaks it down for us in a variety of ways, only one of which I will quote: "For the price of one jet fighter (twenty million dollars) one could set up about forty thousand village pharmacies". So one could go on, quoting from this sombre but not hopeless essay. It is familiar ground for those of us who have read Barbara Ward and René Dubois's *Only One Earth: The Care and Maintenance of a Small Planet*[10] and Gordon Rattray Taylor's books, such as *The Biological Time-Bomb*,[11] *The Doomsday Book*,[12] *Rethink*[13] or *How to Avoid the Future*.[14] The Brandt Report has behind it the authority of a Commission of eighteen international statesmen and leaders from many spheres, and their warnings and recommendations can go unheeded only at our peril. Theirs is indeed a world perspective.

Again and again, as I read that Introduction, I heard the echoes of Biblical truths. The emphasis on mankind as "a single community" echoes the Biblical "God has made of one blood all nations of men for to dwell on the face of the earth",[15] and the vision of St. Paul of God's reconciliation of the whole universe to himself.[16]

"The Commission did not try to redefine development, but we agreed . . . that the focus has to be not on machines or institutions but on people." (Page 23.) The Bible, and especially the Gospels, are full of emphasis on the divine love and compassion for the individual from the call of Abraham to the parables of the lost sheep and the prodigal son.

"If reduced to a simple denominator, this Report deals with peace"; and it is clear that the members of the Commission meant by "peace" not only the end of armed conflicts but also the avoidance of chaos resulting from "mass hunger, economic disaster, environmental catastrophies, and terrorism". Here is something surely very closely akin to the Biblical concept of *shalom*, in the sense of life lived in its fulness (even if the upward dimension of peace with God, dominant in the Bible, is lacking in the Report).

The stress on the perils consequent on ravaging Nature's resources points us to the Judaeo-Christian doctrine of creation and of man as put in trust with its treasures as God's vice-gerent – the *humanum*, that which distinguishes man most closely from the other members of the animal world being precisely his ability to respond, his "responsibility" to the God who created him and trusted him.

"We want to make it quite clear that North and South cannot proceed with 'business as usual' only adding a few bits here and there. What is required is intellectual re-orientation, serious steps toward structural change, increased practical co-operation." Is not that getting pretty close to what the Bible means by *metanoia*, repentance, a change of direction, a change of outlook resulting in a change of action? And is not *metanoia* called for not only on the part of individuals but of nations? Will there not, according to St. Matthew 25, be a judgment of *nations* as well as of individuals, and will it not be based very largely on the kind of issues which confront a "North" nation when it faces the needs of a "South" nation? "The United States", says the Report, ". . . has substantially reduced its international development efforts." And what are we to say about Britain? The response to the Brandt Report by the British Government has not been exactly ecstatically enthusiastic – Edward Heath's realistically warm support has been applauded widely in the country but not by the government. And that same government's withdrawal of grants to overseas students may in the short term slightly help us in our financial distress, but may, in the long term, be seen to be an act of great folly, if only because it is an invitation to tomorrow's leaders to seek their help from (and so give their allegiance to) the countries of the Communist world. "Let us first get straight on the home front and then we may consider world need" can well reflect an insularism which, while regrettable, was understandable a century ago but in the late twentieth century can only be the outcome of blind folly.

To look out on our world with the Brandt Report in one hand and the Bible in the other is to catch a glimpse from the Report of the insights of a group of highly experienced men of the world as they wrestled with its griefs and sorrows, and at the same time to see how immensely relevant are the truths of the Christian revelation in its bearing on those problems. The application of these truths to the present situation faces all concerned with problems of extraordinary complexity, and much of that task must be left to the experts. But the task of the Church in the proclamation of those truths and in the enunciation of their relevance to life is clearly a matter of great urgency. Here in our "Jerusalem", our home base, our London, our New York, we have to look out on the world with the kind of realism which marked Isaiah or Jeremiah or Habakkuk as they surveyed the seething nations of their day, and at the same time we have to indicate the bearing on our situation of our belief in the God of creation, redemption and renewal. Such a task can only be carried out in a spirit of real humility – we are not financiers or economists or (most of us) politicians or scientists; these are skills which others have acquired, and we have no more right to pontificate in these fields than has the Christian priest, engaged on a healing ministry, the right to interfere with the work of the doctor. But that humility does not mean timidity, nor does it imply silence. The Christian voice sorely needs to be heard, provided that voice speaks with the hard-won authority which comes from prayer, study, reading, waiting on God, and contact with men.

An army of educators is called for, and I use the word "educators" in its widest sense. I mean the professional educationists in universities, colleges and schools, of course. I mean the clergy, professionally trained with an expertise all their own, of course. But I refer also to lay men and women, in every walk of life, who in their daily contact with people will help them to "think big", to penetrate behind the obvious and the trivialities of the media to the essential issues, and who will act as gadflies to the consciences of their contemporaries. To many of those contemporaries, the Third World (or the South as we have been calling it) is so dim a reality as to be almost non-existent in their thinking, and to think of the Bible as having any bearing on *The Economist*, or vice-versa, is a concept which has never occurred to them.

I recall a recent visit to the States, to an area which was

very rich in oil and cattle; my friends there did their sums in millions of dollars. But to speak to them of Calcutta, of malnutrition affecting a thousand million people, of appalling population explosions, and to relate these problems to the faith which they professed was to open up an almost new world – and one which proved very uncomfortable! *Here* is our field of activity – to bring pressure to bear on the consciences of our friends, to work for pressure at local government level and to extend that pressure to the spheres of top political involvement.

I do not mean that we should constantly be preaching "political" sermons, still less that we should be telling our people how to vote in any given election. But I do suggest that we should so think and pray and speak that the word of God is enabled to have free course, to penetrate the consciences of men and the structures of society, to leaven the very soggy lump of a people bombarded with news, with facts often distorted by the media, and with heresies which range from the ridiculous to the highly pernicious.

I have mentioned the media. Dr. G. C. L. Bertram, of St. John's College, Cambridge, in a recent letter to *The Times*, spoke of the tremendous significance of "the increase of communication worldwide". There were two consequences to that, he said, one good, the other bad. The first, the good consequence, is that ignorance turns to knowledge, then to sympathy, concern, altruism, and then, maybe, to "a genuine bond of felt love", social service, and aid. The second consequence, the bad one, is that ignorance turns to awareness, jealousy, greed for exaggerated material possessions and supposed well-being – in short (though Dr. Bertram did not add this) to a gross distortion of values. Amid this labyrinthine maze, it is the task of the Christian steadily to guide, direct, point the way, beginning at Jerusalem (wherever we now are) and looking out over the world with eyes made clear by the Spirit of truth.

That guidance, it need scarcely be added, must be given against the background of our own life-style of simple living. "Beginning at Jerusalem", we are en route to the new Jerusalem, the heavenly Zion. It is best to travel light, particularly as we are followers of One who was laid "in borrowed stable and in borrowed grave". It is for us to walk the tight-rope of recognising on the one hand that God "has given us richly all things to enjoy"[17] and we therefore adopt an attitude of affirmative gratitude for all the lovely things of life; and on the other hand that there is a "theology of enough" which finds its joy in a simplicity of life-style and in a sharing of resources. Representatives of twenty-seven countries met last year for an international conference on simple life-style. They issued a statement which included this searching sentence: "It is impossible with integrity to proclaim Christ's salvation if he has not evidently saved us from greed, or his lordship if we are not good stewards of our possessions, or his love if we close our hearts against the needy".

Perhaps, as this lecture has gone on, we have begun to catch a vision of a stream of men and women beginning their witness at "Jerusalem", stripped of any kind of *hybris*, awake to the interdependence of North and South alike in matters economic and ecclesiastical, armed with a world perspective, prophetic insight and speech, marked by simplicity of life-style. Such men and women, in the words of Simon Barrington-Ward, "bring to bear upon this world a love with its eyes open, a shrewd innocence, a resolute fusion of justice and mercy, the very love with which they have been loved".[18] It is a good vision! That vision could, however, be vitiated if we were to become victims of what I might call the menace of mathematical intimidation. That menace may hit us at any number of points. Let me mention two. *First*, our contemplation of the universe as scientists are disclosing it to us can be a chilling experience. A hundred thousand million stars like the sun in the Milky Way and, says Sir Bernard Lovell, "no sign of any end to this immense structure". Who am I and what is my mission in this vast immensity? A speck on a speck, a breath, a tiny candle soon to gutter out! But to reason thus is to shut one's eyes to the teaching of Jesus about the Abba-God, and to think of him as a managing director of a great firm who cannot be bothered with the affairs of the office-boy, still less with the fall of a sparrow. And so to think is to strike at the heart of the Christian revelation.

Secondly, this menace of mathematical intimidation may strike us when we consider the immensity of world need and of world suffering. I will not trouble you with figures – you know the situation well enough. Over against the hopelessness which such a vision might induce in us we can set several positive considerations: the Brandt Report, which approaches world problems not from a theological but from a governmental and economic viewpoint, has in its Introduction these words: (The critical issues facing mankind) "are not hopeless, if decision-makers of the world lend their weight to the solutions . . . Hope itself is the most important element in overcoming obstacles which otherwise might seem insurmountable."[19] Those are the words of a hard-headed realist writing in December 1979, not of a man of 1900 imbued with the ideas of the inevitability of progress. Garth Lean, in his book on William Wilberforce, refers to this "intimidation" as the "helplessness syndrome" which, he says, "is particularly cruel because it drains the meaning out of life. Without vision the people perish, sunk into a slough of comfort, frustration or self-concern. Much of the mindless violence of our time stems from this sense that nothing constructive can be done."[20] The pages of history are bestrewn with instances of the power of minorities, the "success" of men and women of vision and determination. And the history of the Christian Church illustrates in generation after generation the truth of the prophet's word: "not by might nor by a host but by my Spirit, says the Lord".[21]

One recent illustration must suffice. *The Times*, in a recent leading article,[22] drew attention to Dr. and Mrs. Coleman and Miss Jean Waddell who were held captive in Iran for some five months. In particular, it noted a brief message from Dr. Coleman which was played on the radio – "those who heard it can hardly have been other than moved by it." The writer of the article commented:

> These were the accents of calm sincerity, of a faith that is not a matter of sentiment but of plain and all-important fact, of a confidence that there is more to be done as an instrument of God's work in the world. There was no sound of accusation or rancour in the words, only the sound of a sure sanity of mind. It is a sound that penetrates more deeply than that of the largest and most lethal terrorist bomb. It carries the conviction that the forces of darkness will not extinguish the forces of light.

Recent theology has done much to rescue the word "hope" from the inferior position which it has for long held in the Biblical trinity of "faith, hope and love", and we have learnt something new of the meaning of "the God of hope" who with infinite patience and despite all human setbacks works out his pattern in the tangled web of history. To put your hand into the hand of that God is to find yourself linked to a love which cannot be defeated and, "beginning at Jerusalem", you can go anywhere in quiet confidence and steady hope.

4
Out to Latin America

WHEN WE SPEAK of Latin America, we speak of something so vast that it is difficult, especially for us who live on a tiny island, to conceive of it. The geographers tell us that the whole of Africa, that great sprawling continent, Africa, is eleven and a half million square miles in extent. South America alone is nearly seven million square miles, and that, of course, excludes Mexico (which is included when we speak of Latin America). But it is not merely its geographical size which we find it difficult to envisage. To get some mental picture of it, we must think of a variety of nations seething with political unrest, of populations growing at a terrifying rate, of conurbations (with all the problems that belong to that modern form of living) growing at a similar rate, of new cities springing up (Brasilia did not exist a couple of decades ago) and so on. If you want to think in religious terms rather than geographical or political ones, the Readers Digest Great World Atlas will tell you that the Roman Catholic Church in Central and South America has two hundred and forty-four million adherents (a third of the world's Roman Catholics) and the Protestant Churches eleven millions. But of that more anon.

I have called this lecture "Out to Latin America". Why

"out to"? The answer is not far to seek. Let me put it personally. If you were suddenly called on by the Vicar of your Church to give a missionary address – and here I must regretfully assume that the Vicar still uses the word "missionary" in the sense of "having to do with the spread of the Gospel outside these islands" – where would your mind immediately turn to? In nine cases out of ten (perhaps ninety-nine out of a hundred) it would turn to Africa or Asia. Leaving out China, where missionary work has been forbidden for the best part of your lifetime, Africa and Asia have been the two great continents into which the Churches of the West have poured their resources of manpower and money for the best part of two hundred years – often with immense results. To press the point, if you were the one in ten, or one in a hundred, who decided to make Latin America the subject of your address, I think that, except in a comparatively few parishes, you could be pretty sure of virgin soil into which to plant the seed of your address. Still, even today, Latin America is, for the majority of our Church people, *terra incognita*. In the words of St. James, though in a different context, I can only say: "My brethren, these things ought not so to be."

In addressing such an audience as this, I shall wish to speak with some care of the contribution of the Anglican Communion to Christian witness in Latin America. But it would be foolish to attempt even this unless something were first said about the history of Christianity in these countries and about the present position of the Roman Catholic work there and that of many Protestant Churches and sects.

Let us begin with 1492 – that is the date given for the discovery of the new world by Christopher Columbus. The next century was not very old before there was vigorous missionary activity in territories occupied by the Spanish and Portuguese. It was the Orders, led by the Franciscans, who took the lead. Thus, twelve Franciscans arrived in Mexico in 1526; within thirty years there were three hundred and eighty of them, together with two hundred and ten Dominicans and two hundred and twelve Augustinians. It was claimed – with what validity or accuracy it is impossible to say – that within about half a century of the arrival of the Franciscans some five million natives had been baptised.

But before we get too excited about these achievements we must remember that the crown was the power behind the Church and conversion was an element of the conquest. Force, cruelty and greed all had a share in the process of "conversion". In Mexico there were six major languages and many minor ones, so much of the preparation for baptism (where there was any of a serious nature) was done under great difficulty. One Luis Caldera, a Franciscan, who spoke only Spanish, was ingenious enough to overcome his lack of linguistic knowledge when seeking to teach the doctrine of hell: he threw dogs and cats into an oven and lit a furnace under it. The Indians were no doubt duly impressed when they heard the animals scream.

Though there were others more sensitive than Luis Caldera, men who sought to understand the local culture and native ways of thought and of religion, they were often looked upon with suspicion by the Holy Office. Indeed in 1565 the Mexican synod forbade the Indians access to the Scriptures in any language. We see at work in Latin America a process which has bedevilled the missionary work of the Church for many years in many cultures, namely, the imposition of a Western form of Christianity on the people to whom the missionaries have gone, and the identification of Christianity with the national culture of a conquering people. This has meant that the young Church has failed to grow up. It continues to be attached to the apron-strings of its mother. In an ordinary family, it is disastrous to the young when the parents will not let them go. It was a profound psychological insight which made our Lord insist that a man must "leave his father and mother" when he cleaves to his wife.[1] The principle is equally applicable to the younger and older Churches.

Fear led the Dominicans to refuse education and the open Bible to the Indians – fear of resulting heresies. Natives must not be ordained – the fledglings were to be guarded, it was risky to let them fly by themselves! The result in Latin America was, as it has been in many other places, a failure to produce a self-sustaining Christianity – a "foreign" form of Christianity had been imported and imposed.

After Christopher Columbus, thirty-three days after leaving Cadiz, reached the island which he named San Salvador (in what we now call the Bahamas), he reported: "I gave myself to them (the 'savages') and took nothing in return. I did this to pacify them, and that they might be led to become Christians. Let Christ rejoice in the salvation of the souls of so many Christians hitherto lost. Let us all rejoice, both for the exaltation of our Faith and for the increase of our wealth." Max Warren, commenting on these words, wrote: "Unfortunately it was the last five words which really excited Europe. Gold very soon took precedence over Gospel" – and he compares David Livingstone's vision, centuries later, of hope for Africa lying in "Christianity and Commerce". In Latin America the alliance of the Church with the conquering power was a highly dangerous one and was to have repercussions which are still felt today. Triumphalism could not be avoided. Warren comments perceptively about the assumptions that Europe and European ways were the acme of civilisation, and that the Christian Faith could only be exported with its European trappings: "It took centuries for this fundamental arrogance to be recognised, even by missionaries. If, today, there are still acute tensions between the Churches of the West and the Churches of the Third World, we need look no further than this arrogance, no less unpleasant when most unconscious, for an explanation."[2]

In trying to assess the state of the Roman Catholic Church today in Latin America, it is impossible to generalise with any accuracy about an area so vast in extent. However, I think it would be true to say that the day when Rome persecuted members of other Christian Churches is now practically over – the fanaticism directed against minority groups which was a very real thing in the earlier decades of this century, if not wholly a thing of the past, is fast dying. I imagine it is the case that the spirit of Vatican II has penetrated the Roman Catholic Church in Latin America patchily – but that would be true in other parts of Christendom also. (Ireland differs from Bec, to take but one example near home!)

There can be no doubt that renewal is penetrating that Church – and we must thank God for it. The charismatic movement has done and is doing its work in many parts. In Argentina, in Cordova city, Roman Catholics are joining with Anglicans, Methodists, Lutherans, Orthodox and the Salvation Army in the work of the Ecumenical Centre, whose vice-chairman (Archdeacon R. Maitland) and secretary (Sylvia Roitberg) are both Anglicans (the office of President is vacant at the time of this lecture). This venture is a centre of social concern, part of whose work is the difficult task of the rehabilitation of prisoners. It is also a place of study.

Our Bishop in Argentina and East South America with the Falkland Islands, Bishop Richard Cutts, told me last month that he feels that a real beginning has been made in friendship between the Roman Catholic Church and the Anglican. How far that goes in deep ecumenical discussion, in common worship, and reciprocity of function between the Churches is more difficult to say. But again, these same questions have to be asked here at home as well – that is not ecumenism which gets little further than a state of *bonhomie* and does not penetrate to the big questions of doctrine and of reciprocity of Orders. It is at this point, I think, that the Churches now stand in danger. We must not rest on our oars content with a happy state of camaraderie!

We have noted the long and close association of the Roman Catholic Church with the rule of the Portuguese conquerors, and the dangers inherent in such an association. But there is something worse than this which must be noted, if we are to understand what is going on in the Church in Latin America today. Stephen Neill, in his *Colonialism and Christian Missions*, points out that "accurate figures relating to the slave-trade are hard to come by . . . But . . . it seems probable that about five thousand slaves left Angola (in south-west Africa) for Brazil every year for two hundred years." (A very much smaller number than that reached Brazil, because hundreds of them, of course, died of plague during the voyage.) He goes on: "The long acceptance of slavery by the government, *and the acquiescence of the missionaries in it without protest, even when they themselves were not engaged in the traffic*" (italics mine) "undermines the Portuguese claim to have stood for equality between the races". "When slavery was at last abolished by a decree passed in 1858, which, however, was not finally to come into effect until 1878, its place was taken by forced labour."[3] It is a sad story and it brings us relatively close to modern times.

It is not necessary in a lecture such as this to go into the governmental policies of any of the twenty nations that go to the make-up of the great South American Continent today. We know, from a reading of our papers and from such a book as Sheila Cassidy's *Audacity to Believe*,[4] something of the conditions which obtain in countries such as Chile. But, in attempting to assess the significance of the voices which cry out for "liberation" and the writers in Latin America who propound "liberation theology", it is necessary to bear in mind not only the present-day inhumanity of man to man but also the long and tragic story of oppression which I have touched on in mentioning such things as slavery and the Church's acquiescence in it.

Dom Helder Camara has since 1964 been Archbishop of Olinda and Recife. Recife is the capital of the State of Pernambuco and of the north-east region of Brazil. Let me quote him: "We Christians in Latin America have been, and are, seriously responsible for the situation of injustice that exists in this continent . . . In practice, don't we seem to have vindicated Marx by offering to pariahs a passive Christianity, alienated and alienating, justly called an opium for the masses?". If you want to understand what it is that makes this man "the most eloquent witness to the monumental conflict that is taking place in Latin America between 'Christian order' and the Gospel", let me commend to you Dom Helder Camara's *The Conversions of a Bishop: An Interview with José de Broucker*.[5]

If you want to go further and penetrate more perceptively into the power of liberation theology in action at its best, let me further commend to you *Charismatic Renewal and Social Action: A Dialogue*.[6] In this slim volume the greatest figure in the charismatic movement in the Roman Catholic Church enters into conversation with one of the greatest "grass roots" exponents of "socially-committed" theology and praxis. "In our view", writes Cardinal Suenens in the preface, "a Christian who is not charismatic – in the full sense of the word, that is to say open to the Spirit and docile to his promptings – is a Christian forgetful of his baptism. On the other hand, a Christian who is not 'socially committed' is a truncated Christian who disregards the Gospel's commandments." In this book the charismatic leader and the bishop of the poor, "who spends many hours of the night in prayer and is ever conscious of the link between God's ascendancy and his own action", play a kind of duet. They are living examples of men who are determined never to put asunder what God has joined together – spiritual renewal and social commitment. I jotted down here some excerpts I made from Camara. He talks about "the atom bomb of squalid poverty". He talks about "dire poverty which is revolting and degrading; it taints the image of God in every man", and about "the egoism of the rich (which) presents a more serious problem than Communism".

What is liberation theology *about*? When it is realised that half the world's Roman Catholics live under the domination of intolerable dictatorships, it is small wonder that men like Bishop Francisco Claver, S.J., wax wrathful about people who "can worry about relatively piddling things like clerical garb, communion in the hands, correct liturgical vestments and gestures, and other such minutiae, but not unjust wages, government by decree, farcical referendums, lack of due process, torture of prisoners – events that affect people's lives most intensely". Liberation theology, at its truest and best, begins with a healthy doctrine of creation and with a realisation of the fact that the name of Joshua-Jesus comes from a verb whose root meaning is "to be spacious". It must, therefore, find itself in opposition to anything that makes men and women live cramped lives, which blocks them off from being proper human beings. Liberation theology refuses so to "spiritualise" the Gospel as to neglect the physical conditions under which men live or to fail to dig down to the roots that give rise to such conditions. It cannot but have a political orientation, for politics is the field in which the things get done which ruin men, or, alternatively, which make it possible for them to live as children of the Most High. It holds that God, the God and Father of our Lord Jesus Christ, is concerned with the glaring injustice, widespread poverty and sub-human conditions which exist in almost every one of the Latin American countries. (Have you ever seen a favella, or smelt it?)

Gerard Noel, in his book *The Anatomy of the Catholic Church*,[7] has a chapter entitled "Liberation". He vividly depicts the difficulty in which the Roman Catholic Church finds itself when it comes in contact with the governments of the nations which allow such conditions to exist – and "the Vatican maintains full diplomatic relations with each of the countries in question." He gives some terrifying figures about conditions in Argentina, in Bolivia, in Brazil, in El Salvador. With reference to the last of these countries, he refers to General Romero's régime and his "private army of terrorists who, having cut their teeth on the massacres of farmers and students, now terrorise the country at will." He refers to the heroic Archbishop Romero and his cry: "In God's name, we call in the midst of anguish for peace and unity." He wrote just too soon to be able to refer to the martyrdom of that same heroic Archbishop while he was saying Mass in his cathedral at Easter, 1979.

Noel is deeply concerned that within the Roman Catholic Church there is a mighty battle raging. One army defends the "traditional" Western theology and keeps the liberation theologians at bay, scenting Marxist infiltration. The other army, basing its action on views which it traces back (though with varying measures of success) to the Biblical doctrines of God, of Christ, of the Church, of sin, of the consummation of all things, finds itself in the thick of world events in a fight for truth and justice, in an attempt to bring hope to the despairing. Each army, of course, looks wistfully to the Pope, to derive from his utterances (for example, during his visit to Mexico in January 1979 and especially his speech which opened the third Conference of Latin American bishops at Puebla) corroboration for their point of view. Each army hopes to pick up some golden nugget which will support them. Noel points out that there were some strange omissions in that speech – no mention of the persecution of the Church in some of Latin America's Fascist countries; no mention of the eight hundred or so priests who had been imprisoned, tortured or killed in the previous ten years in Latin America, and so on. On the other hand, some bishops of the outlook of Archbishop Romero expressed themselves happy that the Pope had given his support to the protection of human rights and human dignity. Subsequent utterances of the Pope would seem to indicate that he is at pains to rebuke both the luxurious waste and callousness of the West and the conditions which dehumanise so many millions in the Third World (or should we say the Two-thirds World?).

Hans Küng puts the matter of the Church and liberation, and the Church and liberation theology, well in his book *On Being a Christian*.[8] "There must be a commitment to liberation for all who are legally destroyed as human beings or who have no real opportunity to be Christians: for the forsaken of a continent, . . . for the classes of people directly or indirectly exploited . . . Under these specific Latin American conditions *theology* has a special function . . . In such a theology the start should be made not from what theologians have said about theology but from what reality itself says today directly of men and society . . . a 'theology of liberation' presented in the form of a program with great spiritual depth and evangelical immediacy . . . a theology turned against all brutal oppression, whether politico-social . . . erotic-sexual (woman treated as sex object) or pedagogical." That is well said.

Most of the main-line Churches are at work in Latin America. Obviously the Roman Catholic Church has by far the largest number of adherents, but the Orthodox, the Methodists, the Lutherans, the Disciples of Christ, the Waldenses and many others are represented there. Of the Anglican contribution I shall have something to say before I close. But here I must say a word about Pentecostalism. This flourishes mostly in Chile and Brazil – and "flourish" is the right word if we are to judge by the number of people, often poor and forsaken, who come under its influence.

The growth of Pentecostalism, for example in Brazil, has been spectacular. It began about 1910 and it drew its adherents largely from the "lower strata" of society, including those of mixed race and Indians. It has been reckoned that a thousand people a day are converted to Protestantism, which in Brazil means almost exclusively Pentecostalism. (I draw these figures from Walter J. Hollenweger's interesting section on Brazil in his book *The Pentecostals*.[9]) Speaking generally, the Assemblies of God have been suspicious of ecumenism, as represented by the World Council of Churches and by the Vatican Council, on grounds of what they consider to be "apostasy" and "idolatry". It should, however, be added that the W.C.C. is now taking the Pentecostalist phenomenon seriously and is in real dialogue with its leaders.

The rapid growth of this Pentecostal movement is understandable from many points of view. The uninhibited exuberance of worship, its physical expression, its music, its sense of belonging to a great family, its breaking free from what they would call priestcraft, its emphasis on healing and on speaking in tongues – all these things combine to give a sense of relief and release to a people whose lives at best are drab and at worst sordid and dominated by fear and starvation. To belong to such a movement is to feel that the individual matters. It is to be swept up into something which the State certainly does not provide and the main-line Churches regard with suspicion.

It is easy to criticise the Pentecostal movement. To us middle-class and comfortable Anglicans it appears to be over-emotional. Maybe it is – but we Anglicans must ask ourselves whether we have not starved ourselves emotionally when our emphasis has been almost entirely on the intellectual and the volitional. We have never been cold and hungry and lived in a favella. They have – and under these conditions *warmth* is desideratum number one. Against many points of doctrine we should wish to place a question mark, not least on their absence of any clear doctrine of Church Order. But it is to be hoped that, now that closer contact with the World Council of Churches and with the Vatican is a reality, not to say with ourselves, the necessity for Church structure may become more obvious. In this give and take of theological dialogue, the Pentecostalists will doubtless learn from others. It is urgent that we should be humble enough to learn from them.

We have seen something of Roman Catholicism in Latin America – a Catholicism wrestling with the problem of a desperate shortage of priests (though, even so, the Latin American continent has about one hundred and seventy thousand religious – one hundred and forty thousand nuns and thirty thousand male religious – and eight hundred bishops). It is a Roman Catholicism wrestling with a past failure in becoming a Church *of the people* because the vast majority of its priests are foreigners, and with a tension between those who are for and those who are against the demands of the "liberation" theologians. We have seen something of the power and attraction of Pentecostalism in its wide variety of manifestations. We have noted the presence, in varying degrees, of the other main-line Churches. And we should note that the name of the sects is "legion, for they are many"!

Where, in this welter, stands Anglicanism? There were those – and I heard their voices at the 1968 Lambeth Conference – who held that we have no place there. Maybe there are some who still hold that view. I am not one of them.

Let me here interpolate a very brief word on what the present situation is in regard to the Anglican presence in Latin America. The Episcopal Church of the United States of America is mainly responsible, through Province IX, for the work in Mexico (three dioceses), Guatamala, El Salvador, Honduras, Nicaragua, Costa Rica, Panama, Colombia, Equador, Puerto Rico and the Dominican Republic. Venezuela comes under the Province of the West Indies. Brazil, with its five dioceses, is a Province in itself. It is expected that in 1982 another Province will be formed, consisting of the dioceses of Argentina and East South America with the Falkland Islands, North Argentina, Paraguay, Chile and Bolivia, and Peru. That is, in a word, the present "geographical" position.

Historically, it was as long ago as 1825 that an Anglican priest, sponsored by the Bible Society and S.P.C.K., started work in Buenos Aires, Argentina, and four years later the government gave a piece of land for the building of a church which eventually became the pro-Cathedral and is now the Cathedral. In 1869 Bishop Stirling became the first Bishop (Bishops Every, Weller, Evans, Cyril Tucker and now Richard Cutts have been his successors). Mention should also be made of the work of a retired naval officer, an Anglican, Captain Alan Gardiner, who founded a mission on the cheerless shores of Patagonia, and on his third visit in 1850 starved to death with his companions.[10] In recent years there has been a great increase in our work through the labours of the South American Missionary Society: the extension of their work during the General Secretaryship of Canon Harry Sutton (1959–74) is one of the sensational stories of missionary endeavour in this century.

Officially, the Anglican Communion has made its position clear at the Lambeth Conferences of 1958 and 1968. In 1958 I was a member of the Conference when it considered *Progress in the Anglican Communion* and, within that section, of the Committee which considered *Missionary Appeal and Strategy*. We said this about South America: "The Committee believes that so far as the Anglican Communion is concerned, South America is 'the neglected continent', while it is equally a continent of increasing importance in the world today . . . In a few areas the Church is well established, but in most of the continent very little is being done. The little-known and uncivilised tribes of the interior call for pioneer evangelistic work. Vast masses owe no definite allegiance to the Roman Catholic Church and are a prey to materialism or to distorted forms of the Christian faith. South America offers a challenge and opportunity to the Anglican Communion as a great field for evangelistic work." That is what we said in 1958, and we underlined it in 1968. Between the 1958 and 1968 Lambeth Conferences there occurred the first full-scale consultation of "interested parties" at Cuernavaca in Mexico in 1963, which was followed in 1966 by a further consultation in São Paulo, Brazil. I was present at both consultations. This was a new happening within Anglicanism.

If it is asked why Anglican work in Latin America should be increased, it must be made clear that we are not there to proselytise. We are there to evangelise, and there is a limitless field waiting to be entered. But we are also there for another reason: we believe that there are those whose spiritual needs cannot be met either by the Roman Catholic Church or by the Pentecostalist Churches – people who need for their spiritual welfare and succour that combination of liturgical order with freedom which Anglicanism at its best offers, and that balance of word and sacrament which it seeks to present. (There are areas of work where this balance is not being very clearly shown, and where there is a certain "sitting loose" to Church Order, but I speak of what Anglicanism stands for and to which it must ceaselessly strive to attain.)

It has often been said that Anglicans are better at reaching the middle class than they are at reaching the less privileged. This has been held against us almost as a reproach. But may it not well be the case that such people are, in fact, in the Latin America of our day some of the most spiritually needy? The Pentecostals are reaching great numbers of the very poor. Liberation theology is making their needs known and their voices heard – so are the voices of men like Archbishop Helder Camara. Good. But what of the middle classes and the rich, the "poor little rich men"? Have they no souls? No spiritual needs? Will they not be the leaders of tomorrow? If God has given to Anglicans a *charisma* to reach such as them, let us exercise that *charisma* with confidence and humility. Dare we think of ourselves as something of a bridge

Church, an interpreter Church, between Roman Catholicism on the one hand and Pentecostalism on the other, exhibiting in our work at once the value of history and tradition, of a deep and strong theology, of a balanced doctrine of Church, word and sacraments, and at the same time a passionate evangelistic desire to reach the untouched from whatever stratum of society they come? I see there a mission great enough to enlist the life service of any soldier of the Cross.

Last month I had a long talk with Bishop Richard Cutts of Argentina. I asked him: "Do you want new recruits, new helpers?" His answer was definitely "yes". "What sort of men and women do you want?" The answer was equally clear: "Men and women of God, of dedication, of prayer. *Humble* people, ready to listen, to adapt to new situations, to serve and not to dominate".

Latin America presents a great field. Any offers?

5
China Tomorrow?

ONE GLANCE AT China today, and it will be readily appreciated that the most significant part of the title of this lecture is the question mark with which it ends. To begin with – how can we conceive of China at all, a country of nine hundred and fifty million people, a fifth of the human race, the oldest living civilisation in the world? The mind boggles. From a *geographical* point of view, China comprises a vast stretch of territory, from the tropical south to the frozen northern border of Russia and the western roof of the world in Tibet. *Politically*, what can we say of a nation with communist principles which is at deep variance with its neighbouring socialist power, Russia? Where lies the future? And what of China's relationship with the Western world? No wonder that Leslie Lyall's book *New Spring in China*, though its title has no question mark on the cover, has one on every page of the book![1] Is this opening up to the West, which is reported in the press and corroborated by many visitors, a temporary thaw, or is it the appearance of spring in very truth? Much depends on the rulers of China today and tomorrow, and who can say, in the maelstrom of world politics, of what calibre or outlook they will be?

Religiously, what can be said? It is the purpose of this lecture, amid all the uncertainties and all the imponderables, to try to say something of value, for, as I have already said, we are dealing with a fifth of the world's population, and for them, as much as for anyone else, Christ died and rose and lives and cares. But in this field, as in others, one can only tread cautiously and seek to peer into the future circumspectly.

But first, let us look at the soil in which, if it is possible, we would sow the Christian seed. And let us remember that we are dealing with a civilisation far more venerable than our own. It probably began around 1500 B.C., not long before Israel came out of Egypt, reaching its first golden age in the sixth and fifth centuries B.C., the period during which Taoism was founded and, later, Confucius taught. Against that kind of background deep respect, not to say reverence, would seem to be called for. The *Great World Atlas*, to which I have previously referred, with a seemly uncertainty says, under the heading *Religions of the World*, that adherents to Confucianism and Taoism "may number three hundred million, mainly in China, Buddhism one hundred million, Islam ten million". It rightly adds: "exact figures unknown". But the figures given provide some idea of the size of the field with which we are concerned.

If the size of the field is enough to give us pause, and the length of China's history is enough to make us comparative newcomers to civilisation duly reverent, the story of our relationship with China is enough to make us penitent. When I say "our relationship" I mean, of course, the relationship of the West, of Europe and of America, but I think particularly of the relationship which Britain has had with China, and especially in recent centuries.

It is known that as early as the seventh to the ninth century there was a Christian presence in China, for the

Nestorians seem to have had success in establishing the Church there. At the end of the fourteenth century the Franciscans arrived by sea and land. But both these attempts at establishing the Church, Nestorian and Franciscan, died away, and China entered on a period in its history when access to foreigners was very difficult. In the sixteenth century the Jesuits provided contact between the West and the Chinese, for men like Matthew Ricci had qualifications in map-making, astronomy, and so on, of which the Chinese were glad to avail themselves. In the eighteenth century the cloud of xenophobia, fear of foreigners, descended on China again, the main fear being that of Russia and her territorial ambitions. China was militarily weak, and at the same time immensely proud, conscious of her age-long civilisation and tending to regard other nations, about whom she had often extremely inadequate information, as barbarians from beyond the seas. With such nations she could scarcely be expected to trade on a basis of equality! Rather, permission to trade must be granted as a favour given by a superior to inferiors. So it was that in the early nineteenth century traders got but a precarious foothold in China. Relations were not helped by the fact that proud Westerners, often as ignorant of Chinese history as the Chinese were of European history, tended to regard the Chinese as barbarians. Conditions for reciprocity of understanding were not exactly ideal! Robert Morrison, the first Protestant missionary, setting out for China in 1807, travelled in an American ship, and was allowed to stay largely because he was useful as a translator. Paid for this work by the Chinese, he was enabled to pursue his great work of translating the Bible and producing a dictionary. But the situation vis-à-vis any foreigner setting foot on Chinese soil, still more any foreigner wishing to live there, and yet still more any foreigner wishing to propagate a way of life which the Chinese could only regard as Western and therefore under grave suspicion, was bound to be tricky and tense.

Few things worse, then, or more likely to jeopardise all relationships, can be imagined than the occurrence of the Opium Wars in the earliest part of the 1840's. The British government in India wanted to continue, and no doubt to increase, the sale of opium to China against the will of the Chinese. The trade had been going on for many years, but in 1838 there was a sharp rise in the amount of sales and the Chinese government determined to end it. The commissioner who was entrusted with the task of putting into effect the will of the government demanded that all stores of opium should be surrendered and that promises should be given not to import any more. Over a million pounds' worth of opium was destroyed.

The trade clearly was a pernicious and disgusting one. Of course, there were great numbers of people in China who wanted to acquire opium, and revenue from its export to China was felt by the government of India to be essential for its prosperity. At home, the young Mr. Gladstone spoke out boldly in Parliament against the abominable trade and against the possibility of war breaking out over such an issue. But break out it did – and China was in no position to win. Hostilities were brief, but the Treaty of Nanking in 1842, which included the ceding of Hong Kong to the British to meet their need of a naval base, left the Chinese deeply insulted and wounded. Max Warren, in his book *I Believe in the Great Commission*, has this sentence: "Perhaps the most pernicious of all forms of colonialism was what Europeans established in China in the form of complete commercial control, without the acceptance of any moral responsibility whatever."[2]

Further hostilities ensued between 1858 and 1860. It is

true that there had been great cruelty on the part of the Chinese towards the British, but the reprisals which the British meted out to the Chinese were of a peculiarly humiliating kind, and included the burning to the ground of the summer palace of the Imperial House. Bishop Stephen Neill in his book *Colonialism and Christian Missions* has described this as "an act of vandalism perhaps unparalleled in British history."[3] The treaties of 1858 and 1860 which followed these sad events gave freedom, among other things, for the profession and propagation of Christianity. It was now legal for Christian missions to pursue their work, but the background to such work could scarcely be called happy!

We need not go further into the sad story of the humiliation of the Chinese in the years that followed by the French, by the Japanese, and by the Russians. Suffice it to say that the foreigner, and especially the missionary, was regarded as a threat, and those Chinese who became Christians were regarded as half-foreigners worshipping a foreign God. No excuse can be found for the fearful Boxer riots of 1900 in which scores of missionaries and hundreds if not thousands of Protestant and Roman Catholic Christians were murdered. But at least we can begin to see something of the causes of irritation and humiliation which burst into flame on that appalling occasion. One of the few gleams of sunshine which emerged from the dark clouds of those days was the refusal of men like Hudson Taylor to seek for any kind of revenge or even compensation.

I hope that this little sortie into history has not wearied you too much. I felt that some such background was necessary if we were to understand the deeply entrenched feelings of a proud people in their contact with the "outsider". Small wonder that there have been long periods of xenophobia in the history of the Chinese people. Small wonder if an intelligent Chinese today asks with some scepticism: "What *is* the faith of these men of the West? What is the connection between gunpowder, opium, retaliation, and all this talk about love?" Add to this the two bloody wars fought out on European soil and in European skies, one group of "Christian" nations at the throats of another group of "Christian" nations. Add to this the dropping, by "Christian" nations, of the atomic bomb on China's neighbour and the obliteration of Hiroshima and Nagasaki. To put it mildly, the West has hardly commended the Gospel of Christ down the long years, and anyway, why cannot the missionaries, when they come, show a united front? Is their Christ divided? Was Wesley crucified for them? Was it in the name of the Pope that they were baptised? Are the Anglicans only right? – some of them seem to give the impression that they think they are!

If I have painted in dark colours the contact of the West with China, let it not be thought that I am unmindful of the superb sacrifice of thousands of missionaries who have given their skills and their very lives for its evangelisation. During the first half of the twentieth century no country received as many Western missionaries as China. China was the "darling" of American missions in particular. Those who have read the lives of men like Hudson Taylor will know something of the quality of dedication which caused hundreds of men and women to give themselves for life-service to a country from which they could in days before air travel rarely, if ever, return home. There is a marvellous passage in a letter from China written by Hudson Taylor to his sister Amelia: "If I had a thousand pounds, China should have it. If I had a thousand lives, China should have them. No! – not *China* but *Christ*. Can we do too much for Him?" Hudson Taylor himself has been called by no less a church historian than the late Professor K. S. Latourette "one of the greatest missionaries of all time."[4] He was a man of ecumenical spirit before that word was used as it commonly is today, a man of originality in initiating new attitudes to mission, a doctor, a translator, an evangelist, an heroic figure in the Church. It is a cause for thankfulness that Dr. A. J. Broomhall is now engaged on the writing of six volumes, which Hodder's are producing, which will not only throw much new light on Hudson Taylor himself and on his colleagues but will also help us to see the present position of the Christian Church there in the perspective of the long history of missionary enterprise.[5] Under Hudson Taylor's leadership, the missionaries penetrated deep into China. They wore Chinese dress. They identified themselves as far as possible with the customs of the people and sought to win their way not by privilege but by love.

The encouragement of indigenisation, that is to say of the creation of a Church which is and is seen to be the Church of the people, is fraught with difficulty but is of immense importance. We have watched this process at work in Africa where, of set purpose and according to plan, the white missionaries have withdrawn from leadership while the people of the country have taken it over. I may instance the Province of the Sudan which I inaugurated in 1976 on a memorable visit. At the turn of this century there were practically no Sudanese Christians. When the Province began its life all four bishops, including the Archbishop, Elinana Ngalamu, were Sudanese. That was a good example of the outward and visible sign of real indigenisation.

That wise and perspicacious Archbishop of Canterbury, Randall Davidson, saw the importance of this in relation to China early in this century. When in 1917 the first Chinese national was appointed a bishop, Davidson insisted that he should make the oath of canonical obedience not to diocesan authorities at home or to him as Archbishop, but to the Anglican Church in China. Further, when in 1928 Bishop Molony of Chekiang wished to resign, Davidson caused him to offer his resignation to the Presiding Bishop of the Anglican Church in China, and, further, he saw to it that Molony's successor was chosen by the Chinese House of Bishops and consecrated in China.[6] Such action went far to ensure that reality was given to the points which that great missionary statesman John R. Mott made in 1926 when he was outlining the marks of an indigenous Church. "It must", he said, "be self-supporting, self-governing and self-propagating." Of these three "selfs" we shall see more later.

The period of the cultural revolution (1966 to 1976) saw the virtual eclipse of all organised religion in China. All Western missionaries had been forced to withdraw. All places of worship had been closed. The native Christians were left to themselves, and information about the state of the Church reaching the West was minimal. From 1949, indeed, when Mao Tse-Tung's forces finally became the masters of China until his death and that of Chou-en-Lai in 1976, "darkness covered the land and gross darkness the people", at least so far as contact with the West, and in particular with the Church of the West, was concerned. Tiny trickles of information seeped through, and there was evidence of an underground Church and of Christ's people meeting in little groups here and there – but not much more.

Since 1976, however, the situation has begun to alter. It would appear that with the end of the Gang of Four's Cultural Revolution that year, a decisive point in the history of China has been reached. Apparently there is now religious liberty for the various religions in China, and cult buildings, destroyed during the Cultural Revolution, are being restored with government aid. (A distinction is made between "main religions" such as Christianity, Islam, Buddhism etc. and what they designate as "feudal superstition", among which they include sorcerers, divination, praying for sons and daughters(!), controlling demons, healing sickness, etc.) It must be understood that religious liberty does not include religious instruction to those under eighteen. Meanwhile the propagation of atheism goes on in schools. No Sunday Schools are allowed. People are allowed to worship in churches but, officially, not outside. Straight evangelism, as we know it, is virtually out. Nevertheless, religious liberty is now a reality in a sense that it certainly was not before 1976.

In seeking to give you some impression and understanding of the present position in China, I asked for a talk with the Reverend Harry Wittenbach, and he graciously gave me a long interview in London. He will be known to some of you, but for the sake of those who do not know him, let me tell you something about him. He is a young man of eighty just back from an extensive and intensive visit to China. He himself spent twenty years as a missionary there, followed by another eighteen years on the central staff of C.M.S., and since then he has been a curate in London! (There is a lovely tribute to him in Max Warren's autobiography *Crowded Canvas*.[7]) He spoke to me of China as a young people's country. He told me that there are six hundred and thirty million of its people under thirty. Think of what that means for tomorrow. The government is seriously tackling the population explosion. It would seem that the population rises by at least twelve million a year, thus aggravating the problem of poverty which, by Western standards, affects some eighty per cent of its people. There was a remarkable article in *The Times* recently[8] which noted the determination of China's rulers to slay the monster of population growth. I quote from that article: "Every imaginable social and economic sanction is being imposed to deter parents from having more than one or at the very most two. The plan is to bind as many married couples as possible to a vow that their first child will be their last. If they give an undertaking to this effect, or better still let themselves be sterilised, they will straight away be given material rewards and the child will enjoy every benefit the socialist state can supply."

Wittenbach found no begging in the streets – what a contrast to what one finds in India and other eastern lands! He said there was little *visible* poverty, though there was bad housing to be seen. He said that people looked well fed and were not drably dressed. While there were no luxuries for ordinary people, there could be little doubt that conditions had improved since the death of Mao in 1976. China, he said, was "the most puritanical country in the world". You can be sent to prison for playing mah-jong in public!

Though Wittenbach had had some difficulty in getting into China, once he was there he had a large measure of freedom to go where he wanted and ask questions that were on his mind. He was treated with great courtesy, and people were delighted to find him speaking to them in their own language and answering their questions about a China which, because of their comparative youth, they had never known. He received a great welcome.

Wittenbach insisted that the Chinese must be treated with respect. He quoted a humorous saying of theirs: "The British think they are the superior race. We *know* we are." Anyway, we have seen that their culture antedates ours by many centuries. Understandably enough, the Chinese – and this goes for the Christians as well as others – are suspicious of Western designs upon them. Have they not memories of Western imperialism? Therefore any person, or any Church, or any organisation of the West seeking entry into China must enter at the invitation of the Chinese and with their good will. He came back to that again and again. Without this, the activities of a bull in a china shop would be, in comparison, pacific.

Nor do the Christians in China want a re-imposition of the divisions and denominational differences of the Western Church. Theirs is a post-denominational Church – they have kept the Faith and lost the denominations. To the question: "Which Church do you belong to?" they hardly care to give an answer. Their eyes are on the future, with little interest in the past. (Well, I seem to remember that St. Paul had something to say about that.[9])

Nevertheless, problems surround them, and await them. Wittenbach described them as a first-century Church. But a first-century Church will have to face second-century problems – problems of organisation and structure, of Order, of who celebrates the Eucharist and who baptises, of the Protestant emphasis on word and lack of emphasis on sacrament, and of the Roman Catholic opposite approach to these means of grace. Can they face such problems without lapsing into the tragic brokenness of denominationalism which saps evangelistic energies and weakens witness? How can one be a truly national Church and at the same time make a contribution to the ecumenical Church? How do you live down the old jibe: "When the Church gains a convert China loses a citizen"? How do you give your loyalty to the "Three Self Movement" – self-determination (i.e. Chinese decisions), self-propagation (Chinese manpower) and self-support (Chinese money rather than overseas dependence) which after all, as we noticed, were the marks which John R. Mott expected to see in an indigenous Church – and at the same time give to the ecumenical Church and gladly receive from it?

There is also the old problem of loyalty to God and to Caesar – not easy to resolve when Caesar is Marxism and, in a way, even less easy to resolve when Marxism, in the words of the 1978 Lambeth Conference, "has an attraction for many because it has a passion for people's welfare, a sense of the sins of society and of the powerful – and in these ways it could be said to have the support of Scripture." Leslie Lyall in his *New Spring in China*, writing on the religious character of Marxism, says: "Communism is, of course, a religion not of personal salvation but of collective improvement. Nevertheless, the Christian concepts of redemption, future bliss, struggle with evil, faith and charity are common to Communism. The emphasis on practice as well as theory and on dedicated service to the community are also significantly present both in Christianity and in Marxism."[10]

And again, what do you do with those who "lapsed" during the long weary years of persecution? Has the story of the Donatist controversy in the fourth century in North Africa any lessons to teach the Church in the twentieth century in China? Now that, at least in some areas, churches are being re-opened, what is the position of the house-churches which have sprung up with a mushroom-like growth? Is the latter kind of informal and often unstructured worship adequate, or must some major readjustments be made if the Church of God which is in Chekiang or Shanghai or wherever is to worship and witness as a vital part of the Church Catholic?

The Roman Catholic Church in China has problems all its own since the Patriotic Catholic Association cut ties with the Vatican in the 1950's in order to assert the national and Chinese character of its Catholic faith. Mass is still said in Latin, and it is not to be wondered at if there are signs of a pre-Vatican II form of Roman Catholicism in a Church which was for so long cut off from contact with the West. Wittenbach found the Roman Catholic Cathedral in Canton to be a place of lively worship. It had been destroyed in 1966, every window broken and pews and books made into a bonfire in the middle of the building. Here he found a picture of life, but with adjustments to be made with Rome and relationships deepened with the non-Roman Christians.

If the Chinese Church is willing to be obedient to the Spirit, might it not have a new contribution to make to the ecumenical Church? Might this not be another instance of *ex oriente lux*? A Church which has come through the fires of persecution, a Church which is highly suspicious of the old kind of denominationalism which the West imposed on it, might well be the Church with something new to say to Geneva and to Rome and to Canterbury, if those three ancient bastions would be ready and humble enough to listen.

If aid is to be given from without to China – and here I return after a bit of a digression to Wittenbach – might it possibly be better made from, say, North or South India which have ventured forth into unity while we in the West have dragged our feet? Might not a post-denominational Church be more inclined to listen to another post-denominational Church and to receive help from it, rather than from a Church that is still shackled with the fetters of disunity?

After the Treaty of Nanking had been signed in 1842, China was open in a measure to the Gospel. Of this period Stephen Neill writes: "Societies of many nations and many confessions rushed in through the open door, to take in hand the evangelisation of the empire. They could hardly have done otherwise. Yet, if we take a wider view of the purposes of God, it might have been better had they been content to wait. However innocent the missionary might be of national prejudices and imperialist aspirations, his position in Chinese eyes was, to say the least, ambiguous. . . . "[11] Is this a warning to us, some one hundred and forty years later? There are, as we have seen, signs of a thaw, if not of spring, in China. Can the West help? If so, how? Wittenbach would reply: "Only under certain conditions." For example, any help can only be given on invitation from the Chinese. Bishop Gilbert Baker, who has just retired from Hong Kong to be succeeded by a Chinese, said recently in a letter to me: "Chinese Christians know how quickly Western generosity can turn into Western pressure." Further, any help can only be given with great courtesy (which, after all, is one aspect of love). It can only be given when the giver goes in the form of a servant. Much of it might come better from lay men and women rather than from clergy; there is considerable freedom of movement for businessmen and for those in the diplomatic service, and some openings for English teachers. That is not to say that there will not be any openings for clergy from the West, providing they go under the foregoing conditions. There may be such places, perhaps particularly in the realm of theological education.

Does this all sound rather over-cautious and analytically cool? I think it does. But we must be alert to learn and profit from the past follies which history would teach us. This, however, must be added. There is in China a population which by the end of this century will consist of about a thousand million human beings, the vast majority of whom will not have had the opportunity of any real confrontation with Christ, many of whom will never have heard his name. Anyone claiming the name of disciple must long to reach them, some to go to them in person. What can we do?

(1) We can *pray,* with the kind of informed prayer which we have mentioned before in these lectures. We must pray with the expectancy that recognises that the God of history has a way of doing new things. Cardinal Suenens keeps on speaking about the God of surprises. It may be that we are not only seeing a thaw but a spring which will ripen into summer more rapidly than we can dare to think. We must pray earnestly and expectantly.

(2) We can make a point of *learning* all we can about China, its history and culture, its particular form of Marxism, its developing interest in world religions. The serious newspapers in Europe and North America can often be for us a source of enrichment, for the best journalists realise that China is now an important factor in the world scene. That is something all of us can do.

(3) We can *cultivate friendships* with Chinese living in this country and learn from them, in the intimacy of friendship, much that newspapers and books do not provide.

(4) We can take our part in *encouraging Sinology* in our universities, so that from them there may go out at least a trickle of men and women who are experts in this field. Maybe, who knows, you might be a drop in that trickle. It is at least worth putting up a prayer to the God who has a way of guiding those who want to know his way with their lives.

Postscript to Lecture 5

Various matters have led to a delay in sending to the press, in October, the lectures which I gave in February 1981. News from China continues to reach the West, as any reader of a responsible newspaper can see, though often that news comes in bits and pieces. I thought it worthwhile to add a postscript to this lecture, in order to give certain facts and figures received from a friend who visited China in August of this year. He travelled widely and met many people, including Bishop Zheng, General Secretary of the China Christian Council in Shanghai, and Bishop Ting, President of the Council from Nanjing. I give the information in his own words:

> There are 160 churches open at present in China (I am talking throughout of the United Church and not the Chinese Catholic Church) but Zheng was unable to give me an up-to-date figure for the number of pastors. There must however be at least three hundred as in all the churches I visited there were at least two and in some places four. Congregations are substantial and in Nanjing on Sunday morning there were some seven hundred present; at Hangchow I was told they

have 1,300 for the morning service. Zheng told me that in Shanghai at the five churches now open the total Sunday attendance is 5,000. Many pastors thought dead are reappearing! Bishop Ting told me that when he was able to function again in Nanjing there were twenty-five house groups which made themselves known of whose existence he had previously been unaware.

At Nanjing the Theological Institute has been reopened from February and there are thirty-nine students, of whom nineteen are women. They were selected from 308 applications and come from twenty-two provinces. The total staff there is thirty, of whom twelve are teachers, four being women.

Perhaps the above information should be read in conjunction with the cautionary note which has come from Keston College since my lecture was given:-

USE OF RELIGIOUS BUILDINGS IN CHINA

The China Study Project's regular bulletin "Religion in the People's Republic of China" (Documentation No. 4, Feb. 1981) quotes a report by A.F.P. in English as saying:

> "The Chinese government has decided to allow all religious buildings, with the exception of those being used as factories or schools, to revert to their original functions again, an official said here today (Peking, 23 December 1980). The spokesman for the government's Religious Affairs Bureau said that restoration work would be carried out 'gradually'."

Keston College comments that the use of the term "gradually" is significant, as it is an almost certain indication that the rate of restoration is likely to continue to be extremely slow.

It is known that a great number of religious buildings are presently being used as factories and schools, and such buildings are specifically excepted. The official does not clarify whether churches being used as warehouses are also classed as "factories". Chinese-speaking Western visitors to China in recent months have pointed out that it is extremely difficult to find alternative business premises for concerns presently housed in church or other religious buildings.

At least we may note that Roger Garside's book on *China after Mao*, favourably reviewed in *The Times* of 30 July, 1981, has as its main title *Coming Alive!*

Notes

1 – The Biblical Perspective

1 Hodder and Stoughton, 1963.
2 Blackwell, 1929.
3 16,15.
4 *Into all the World: A Biography of Max Warren*. Hodder and Stoughton, 1980.
5 1 Corinthians 14,8.
6 *Sons of the Prophets: Evangelical Leaders of the Victorian Church*. S.P.C.K., 1979, p. 88.
7 Cambridge University Press, 1926.
8 *Christian Idea of Atonement*, p. 311.
9 Isaiah 63,9.
10 Exodus 19,4.
11 Hosea 11,3–4.
12 S.C.M.
13 Dylan Thomas seemed to be feeling his way towards a belief in a God who suffers when he wrote: "He, on top of the hill in heaven, weeps whenever, outside that state of being called his country, one of his worlds drops dead, vanishes screaming, shrivels, explodes, murders itself. And, when he weeps, light and his tears glide down together, hand in hand" (quoted in Andrew Sinclair's *Dylan Thomas, Poet of his People*, Michael Joseph, p. 158).
14 St. John 1,18.
15 Isaiah 40,5.
16 St. John 3,16.
17 Ephesians 1,9–10.

18 1 Corinthians 15, 25, 28.
19 Romans 11,36, N.E.B.
20 St. John 20,19–23.
21 St. John 12,23 ff.
22 Charles Scribner's Sons, 1975.

2 – A Gospel for *All*?

1 Deuteronomy 7,7 ff.
2 Ezekiel 16,1–7.
3 Isaiah 42,6–7.
4 Isaiah 49,5–6.
5 David J. Bosch: *Witness to the World: The Christian Mission in Theological Perspective*. Marshall, Morgan and Scott, 1980, p.239.
6 St. Luke 4,16 ff.
7 St. John 1,11.
8 *The Ordeal of Love: C. F. Andrews and India*. O.U.P., 1979.
9 St. Luke 1,46 ff.
10 C.M.S. News-letter, October 1980.
11 David J. Bosch, op. cit., pp. 202 ff.
12 Hodder and Stoughton, 1974.
13 Hodder and Stoughton, 1980.
14 Hodder and Stoughton, 1976.
15 St. John 5,17.
16 Acts 17, 26–27.
17 Acts 10, 1 ff.
18 In the Epilogue to her book *Merton: A Biography* (Collins, 1980), Monica Furlong writes that "he knew that something had still eluded him and hoped very much that he would find it in the Asian religious communities. Some Christian observers have seemed to take offence at this . . . But Merton never thought or wrote of ceasing to be a

Christian. Christianity was, quite simply, his language, and could no more be renounced than any native tongue; but this did not mean that other languages might not be loved and yield striking new insights in the old familiar phrases and ideas. In a number of the Buddhist and Hindu teachers Merton met in Asia, he found holiness and a deep knowledge of the realities of prayer, and he was humble enough to listen and to learn." (p. 339).

19 Ephesians 1,22–23.

20 1 Corinthians 15,28 (RSV).

21 Romans 16,26.

3 – "Beginning at Jerusalem"

1 St. Luke 24,47.
2 1 Corinthians 15,14.
3 St. Luke 4,22.
4 *George Macaulay Trevelyan: A Memoir*. Hamish Hamilton, 1980.
5 Weidenfeld and Nicolson, 1979.
6 Philippians 2,8.
7 Quoted in F. W. Dillistone: *Into all the World*, pp. 92–93.
8 Revelation 3,17.
9 Pan Books, 1980.
10 Penguin Books, 1972.
11 Thames and Hudson, 1968.
12 Thames and Hudson, 1970.
13 Secker and Warburg, 1972.
14 Secker and Warburg, 1975.
15 Acts 17,26.
16 Colossians 1,20.
17 1 Timothy 6,17.
18 *C.M.S. News-Letter*, March 1980.
19 p. 25.
20 *God's Politician: William Wilberforce's Struggle*. Darton, Longman and Todd 1980, p.173. Bishop Launcelot Fleming, in an address at Kurt Hahn's funeral, said of that great educator that he saw the young "as exposed to a series of decays – the decay of fitness, the decay of self-discipline, the decay of enterprise and adventure, the decay of skill and

care and, most shattering of all, the decay of compassion . . . With all of this he was conscious of *the disintegrating power of cynicism*" (italics mine). Donald Lindsay: *Friends for Life: A Portrait of Launcelot Fleming*, pp. 248–49. Lindel Publishing Co. 1981.

21 Zechariah 4,6.

22 January 2, 1981.

4 – Out to Latin America

1 St. Matthew 19,5.
2 *I Believe in the Great Commission*, pp. 110–111.
3 1966.
4 Collins, 1977.
5 Collins; first published in Great Britain 1979.
6 *Malines Documents No. 3*. Darton, Longman and Todd, 1980.
7 Hodder and Stoughton, 1980.
8 Collins, English translation 1976. See especially pp. 554 ff.
9 S.C.M., First British edition 1972.
10 The headquarters of S.A.M.S. in Tunbridge Wells is called Alan Gardiner House.

5 – China Tomorrow?

1 Hodder and Stoughton, 1979.
2 p. 113.
3 Lutterworth Press, p.138.
4 *History of Christian Missions in China*, p. 382.
5 *Hudson Taylor and China's Open Century*. Hodder and Stoughton and the Overseas Missionary Fellowship. Book I – *Barbarians at the Gates* appeared 1981.
6 See further G. K. A. Bell: *Randall Davidson, Archbishop of Canterbury*, pp. 1227–1229.
7 pp. 188–189.
8 January 8, 1981.
9 Philippians 3,13–14.
10 p. 240.
11 *Colonialism and Christian Missions*, pp. 135–136.